ON
PUBLISHING

A Professional Memoir

ON PUBLISHING

A Professional Memoir

LIONEL LEVENTHAL

Greenhill Books, London

To
Elizabeth

Greenhill Books

On Publishing: A Professional Memoir
first published 2002
in a limited edition of 750 copies
by Greenhill Books, Lionel Leventhal Limited,
Park House, 1 Russell Gardens, London NW11 9NN

British Library Cataloguing in Publication Data
Leventhal, Lionel
On publishing : a professional memoir
1. Leventhal, Lionel 2. Publishers and publishing – England – Biography
3. Booksellers and bookselling – England – Biography
I. Title
070.5'092
ISBN 1-85367-517-2

Production direction: Hugh Allan
Edited by Kate Ryle
Designed by David Gibbons, DAG Publications Ltd
Typeset in Lucida Bright
This book is printed on Munken Book Extra, vol 18, 80 gsm paper
supplied by Gerald Judd Sales in conjunction with Trebruk UK
Jacket and plates printed on Challenger Art paper supplied by
The James McNaughton Paper Group
Book casebound in unlined greyboard supplied by Doric Board and Packaging
Cover material Wibalin and endpapers Wibalin natural
supplied by Winter & Company
Printed and bound in Great Britain by CPD (Wales),
Ebbw Vale

CONTENTS

	Rules of Engagement	7
	My Kind of Town	9
1	Bookselling Can Kill You	11
2	A Profession for Gentlemen	15
3	The Start of my Military Book Publishing	25
4	With Paul Hamlyn	29
5	Arms & Armour Press: Getting Started	35
6	Arms & Armour Press: The First Offices	41
7	'Hello, English'	49
8	Working with the Soviets, and the Russians	61
9	Going to America	69
10	An American Relationship	75
11	Arms & Armour Press: The Glory Years	81
12	Quality Bookselling	91
13	How the London Book Fair Started	117
14	ABA, BEA and Military Book Show	129
15	Having a Number One Bestseller	139
16	The One that Got Away	145
17	Greenhill Books: The First Decade	149
18	Authors	161
19	Working with Dead Authors	165
20	In Memoriam	171
21	Producing Books	183
22	Special Projects	187
23	Litigation	193
24	The Business of Publishing	199
	Is There a Message?	203
	Index	204

ILLUSTRATIONS

PHOTOGRAPHS

The Herbert Jenkins team,
summer 1964   97

J. Derek Grimsdick   97

The first offices in Childs
Hill, 1969   98

The building of
2-6 Hampstead High Street   98

Richard Brown with Lionel
Leventhal in the Ken
Trotman office   99

The team at Arms & Armour
Press, 1980   99

At the Arms Fair, March 1968   100

The village of Kronberg   100

Mark Wray with Dina and
Eddie Coffey at the
Frankfurt Book Fair   101

Bill Corsa   101

John Taylor   102

Greg Oviatt   102

The Stackpole team at
BookExpo America, 2000   103

James Opie   103

The team at Greenhill Books,
August 2000   104-5

Robert L. Pigeon   106

Colonel Robert and
Mrs. Edie Kane   106

Cecil Lewis in World War One,
and on the re-publication of
Sagittarius Rising with Dr.
Michael Fopp   107

Dr. David G. Chandler   108

Ian Knight   108

John Walter   108

Ian Hogg   109

Chaim Herzog   109

Jeffrey L. Ethell   110

John Elting   110

Edward Ryan   110

Jack Gill   111

Kenneth Macksey   111

Paddy Griffith   111

Peter Tsouras   112

Sheila Watson and
James Lucas   113

LINE ILLUSTRATIONS

The military book triangle   8

The Herbert Jenkins building   16

Starting young   27

The A&AP logo   43

The evolution of the London
Book Fair 1971-1984   122

The Greenhill logo   150

RULES OF
ENGAGEMENT

THIS BOOK IS A LIMITED EDITION and assumes acquaintance with two things: the undersigned, and book publishing. You will also need a certain amount of patience, an interest in yesteryear (for some things seem now to be historic, even quaint, however real, fashionable or up to date they were at the time) and the evolution of modern publishing.

Although this memoir unfolds chronologically, quite a number of subjects are treated thematically, and hence reminiscences about the Frankfurt Book Fair, for example, span from my time with Herbert Jenkins to the present, those about the London Book Fair cover the early 1970s to the present, and the chapter about the ABA (aka BEA) follows a similar pattern. I have also told separately, out of chronological sequence, the stories of special events or circumstances, such as *Who Dares Wins*, *The Hunt for Red October*, working with authors and so forth. Sometimes one returns to the same subject more than once, I hope without exact duplication (although this may depend upon the sub-editing of this little memoir), but there is, overall, a chronological progression notwithstanding the occasional meander.

I have, of course, not been able to mention all of those with whom I have worked over the years, and apologise if your name is one that you might possibly have expected to find and is not here. You are in good company. It has been a privilege to work with so many fine authors, publishers and booksellers and others, around the world and over the years, that I could probably have filled a volume of similar size to this with a listing and bare information.

Lionel Leventhal, 2002

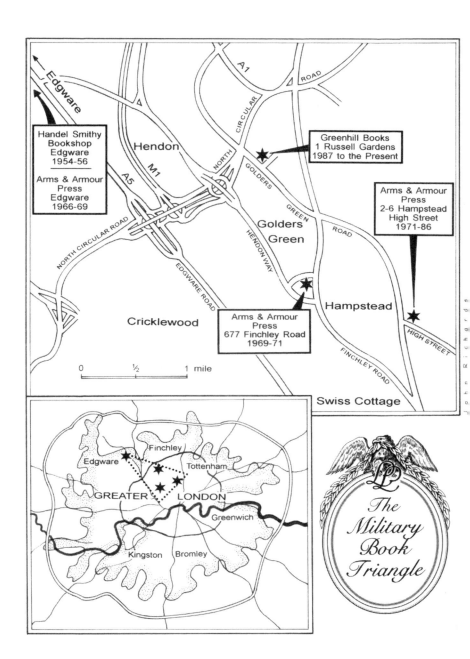

Handel Smithy
Bookshop
Edgware
1954-56

Arms & Armour
Press
Edgware
1966-69

Greenhill Books
1 Russell Gardens
1987 to the Present

Arms & Armour
Press
2-6 Hampstead
High Street
1971-86

Arms & Armour
Press
677 Finchley Road
1969-71

Hendon

Golders
Green

Hampstead

Cricklewood

Swiss Cottage

0   ½   1 mile

John Richards

Finchley

Edgware

Tottenham

GREATER   LONDON

Greenwich

Kingston   Bromley

The
Military
Book
Triangle

MY KIND
OF TOWN

LONDON IS.

My entire career has been in London, and I was very fortunate to start when a small publishing house such as Herbert Jenkins could have its own building, with a trade counter, in St. James's. Those were the days when all publishers were in Bloomsbury or select adjacent environs.

Then came Covent Garden, whilst the food and flower market was still there and before it became fashionable with boutiques and coffee shops.

Hence I got to know these two areas of this great city by working in them, and travelling on foot. When I started working in London in the mid-1950s it still felt like a village, yet it had the solid confidence from having been the capital of an empire. Over the years London has become busier, less gentlemanly and more diverse, and it has become a congested, vibrant and exciting city.

My career in publishing military books has been wholly in North West London. Possibly someone at some future date will notice the North West London addresses, all within a fairly small geographic triangle, on many military books published in the last thirty-five years of the twentieth century (and continuing) and wonder why. The reason has been a very practical one: I have lived all this time a little way to the north of the area in Hertfordshire, and North West London represented a reasonable commuting journey for me and was as far as it was acceptable to expect those with whom we worked, and overseas visitors, to travel.

1

BOOKSELLING
CAN KILL YOU

I BELIEVE THAT I ENTERED PUBLISHING in the best way, from bookselling. I left school aged fifteen years and one week, for the academic (for want of a better word where I was concerned) year ended in June, a week after my birthday. I left with no certificate or academic qualifications, and did a few general clerical jobs before I decided that as I had no career in mind it would be best if I worked in some way in an area I enjoyed. The only thing that I enjoyed was reading. The only jobs mentioned in the career guides that had a relationship with books were librarianship (for which you had to take exams, which did not sound much fun) or bookselling. Hence in the Spring of 1954, when Bill Haley and His Comets introduced the world to rock and roll, I got a job in a bookshop.

My first job in the book trade was at the Handel Smithy Bookshop in Edgware, named after the smithy on the spot where Handel composed *The Harmonious Blacksmith*. The wage was £3.20 per week. Yes, that was the wage per week, not per day or per hour. Saturday was a full working day, but there was a half-day on Thursday. And, no, those were not the days of gaslight, or the penny farthing bicycle.

The Handel Smithy Bookshop was a typical small independent shop. The owner was Gerald Konyn, a wonderful bookman but a bad businessman. He was brilliant as a salesman, and could charm local ladies into buying books they wanted but could not afford. One fine series at that time was the Skira books, the first of a new post-war generation of top quality art books. Those who looked upon them with admiration, but thought that they were out of their financial reach, were soon talked into a 'pay away' plan by Gerald. They loved the books, and loved him for making it possible for them to acquire them. He was truly a bookseller customers could rely upon for recommendations, and at the time that Nicholas Monsarrat's *The Cruel Sea* was a bestseller, in its day without parallel, we were selling to Gerald's regular customers another novel (*The Diplomat* by James Aldridge), which had received no publicity (or ever did), in greater quantity.

Soon after joining the shop I had to go to the warehouse of the bankrupt wholesaler, Simpkin Marshall, to buy books that were being sold off by the receiver. It was this event that sounded the warning to the book trade of Captain Robert Maxwell's way of doing business.

Books that were first published in the mid-1950s, and which were sold before their current fame and critical acclaim, included Tolkien's *The Lord of the Rings,* Golding's *Lord of the Flies,* and the first James Bond books by Ian Fleming. I was able to talk a number of regular customers into buying Tolkien's *The Lord of the Rings,* although at the time there was no precedent for a book about a mythic world. There was indeed quite a remarkable credibility gap, but most of those customers who took *The Lord of the Rings* away were enthralled, and as there was a period of time between the publishing of the various volumes, we received any number of enquiries from impatient customers who were concerned about Frodo left captured by orcs until the next volume came along. Alas, I did not have the foresight to keep first editions of these books; a set of *The Lord of the Rings* sold not so long ago at auction for £11,000.

At the time there was a sensational radio serial called *Journey into Space.* The producer and writer Charles Chilton lived close to the shop, and so too did one of the actors. The shop made an arrangement for an autographing party with the whole cast, and as part of this, in order to set up a display in the shop's window in Edgware's Station Road, the publisher Herbert Jenkins supplied what in the 1950s was regarded as a spaceman's suit. This was a white rubber affair, with rings that needed blowing up with air, plus a glass bubble helmet. This was made for display purposes only, but Gerald Konyn had the great idea that if I were dressed in it, and the suit was inflated, and I walked along Station Road, this would attract considerable attention, press photography, and so forth. He was right. After I had got into the outfit and it was inflated my arms stood out by my sides, away from my body, rather like a Michelin man advertisement. The helmet was put over my head, and affixed by bolts to a ring around the neck of the suit, and I started my walk, or rather waddle, up Station Road. However I soon discovered a little problem. Because the suit had been made for display purposes only there was no air vent to the helmet. And then, because there was no air vent, the air seemed to be getting a little thicker inside the helmet, which started misting up. I started gesticulating towards the helmet, to try to attract attention to this problem, but nobody understood and in fact they thought that my waving of my arms was rather funny, in an alien sort of way. It was only when I lowered myself to the ground and started beating the perspex bubble helmet on the pavement that the crowd realised that I had a problem. This was also a good introduction to the perils of book publicity.

Most unfortunately Gerald Konyn's wife was seriously unwell, and even in those dark days of Cold War he managed to arrange for treatment at a specialist centre behind the Iron Curtain in Hungary. This meant, however, that he was away from the shop for extended periods and he left the running of it in the hands of a callow youth in his very first job in bookselling. Hence I had to take over the ordering of the books, which was a great experience in dealing with sales representatives, and in learning how to control and speed up sales presentations by taking from their hands the sales kit. Those were the days when books were sold to bookshops at $33\frac{1}{3}$ per cent discount, plus carriage, and on a firm basis; 'see safe' (returning some books to the publisher, but replacing them with others of the same value) was a privilege.

The down side, however, was that only Gerald Konyn could sign cheques, assuming that there was money in the bank, and with his extended absences this caused all sorts of problems: another introduction to the problems of commercial life.

I think that getting into book publishing via bookselling should be obligatory for all on the sales, marketing and commercial side of publishing, and probably editorial as well. One learns a great deal from handling books, speaking to the customers, seeing the reactions of customers and understanding their needs. Even after all these years I can still remember customer reaction (such as when the *Guinness Book of Records* was being newly published, and the shop was being used for test marketing), book jackets, and so forth. Another lesson was to have credible acknowledgements and a quality bibliography in non-fiction books. These essentials for the making of good books were learned from sessions I had once a month with the local librarian, who bought the books for three or four public libraries. We held all the new books on one side for him to peruse when the shop was closed on a Thursday afternoon. He could work through several hundred books, deciding very quickly which he wanted and which he did not, and the quantity. Buying fiction was easy, but I asked him how he managed to buy non-fiction so quickly, sorting the books into various quantity categories. 'I always look at the acknowledgements, to see where the author is coming from and where he has undertaken his research', he said, and 'if I see a bibliography is lacking details, or isn't correctly put together, then that certainly shows me straight away that the author hasn't undertaken the right research, and doesn't have a logical approach to things.' These were the first lessons for my career in publishing.

After a couple of years at the Handel Smithy Bookshop I decided to move on, and after having written to many publishers (whose rejection letters I kept and was able to remind some people about in later years) joined Herbert Jenkins, who coincidentally were the publishers of *Journey into Space*.

2

A PROFESSION
FOR GENTLEMEN

THE TERM 'A PROFESSION FOR GENTLEMEN' was used about publishing at the time when I started my first job with a book publisher in the Spring of 1956. I joined Herbert Jenkins, a small general publishing house with offices in Duke of York Street, just off Jermyn Street in London's St. James's. They published fiction for which the main market was libraries, and some general non-fiction, but the firm (and possibly reflecting the whole of British business at that time) was really run as a 1930s business might have been. Indeed all the directors had been with Jenkins since that time. Derek Grimsdick was the managing director, and he and his family owned the company. He had been away during World War II, and served in the Royal Navy on the Arctic convoys to Murmansk. The editorial director was Tom Eagle. He had joined in the 1930s from Hatchards, in the days when shop staff still wore frock coats. Tom was disabled and hence could not serve in the war and was able to maintain the company's publishing during World War II. The production director was Gerry Rees. He had been on holiday in Germany in 1938, and returned to the office forecasting war and a shortage of paper, and hence bought an enormous amount for future printing. This prescience was unfortunately not to the benefit of the company, because the Government pegged profitability of businesses during the war to the 1939 level.

The mid-1950s were still in the recovery period from World War II, before air travel became common, before communications quickened by means of telex (which was many years before fax, and now e-mail), when public library business was substantial, books were printed by letterpress and all sales were firm. If the directors who ran Herbert Jenkins, and who were so kind to and tolerant of me, were to return they would not recognise the modern book trade.

I joined as an Editorial Assistant and on my first day was given a book of crosswords to sort out. The problem was that

The Herbert Jenkins building at 3 Duke of York Street, off Jermyn Street in London's St. James's.

the copper blocks for the crossword grids had been made for all the puzzles without a puzzle reference number. On the other hand all the questions and answers had been typeset, also without puzzle reference numbers. Somebody had to join them together, and that was me. It was an effective way of giving a new member of staff a job that would keep him quiet for a period.

The Herbert Jenkins backlist included many books from before World War II, including a range on Scouting. The sales had in fact slowed, and decisions had to be made as to what to keep in print. From those innocent days there was one book called *Things to do in the Woods with Brownies*, and that was one title they decided to drop. Authors I worked with included Victor Silvester and Andre L. Simon, and others well known in the 1960s (but possibly only nowadays to specialist book collectors). One of the things I was appointed to do after I had been there for a few years was to expand the non-fiction list, which led Jenkins to publishing books about firearms, and the fine *Victorian Collector Series*. I also added science fiction to their publishing, and published the Michael Moorcock book *Stormbringer* (1964) and others by such authors as E. C. Tubb (Cordwainer Smith wasn't available). I arranged the publication of some novels that tied in with TV series, such as *Bonanza*, but there was no market for such; who would want to read what was seen on television?

A mainstay of Jenkins, at least where reputation was concerned, was P. G. Wodehouse, whom they had published since shortly after World War I. At that time, however, sales of new Wodehouse books were modest, for the reaction to his wartime broadcasts from Germany had been extremely negative. Jenkins even arranged for these innocuous, subtly anti-Nazi broadcasts to be published in the Penguin edition of one of his volumes of autobiography (*Performing Flea*, 1961) but this did little to assuage the damage, which only time could heal and this took another decade or two.

I did not personally liaise with Plum (as Wodehouse was called), for he had a long-standing relationship with two of the directors. Hence when I made my first visit to the United States for Herbert Jenkins in 1961 I turned down the offer to go to

Plum's Long Island home to meet him. I had something of a blind spot for his books and was afraid of upsetting the relationship. During this visit, however, I met David A. Jasen, the American who was to write *P. G. Wodehouse: The Portrait of a Master* (1975), *A Bibliography and Reader's Guide to the First Editions of P. G. Wodehouse* (1970; second edition Greenhill, 1986), etc., and was able to share with him all sorts of information from our files, and obtain for him on the second-hand market first editions of many books.

My Wodehouse relationship does include creating a particularly rare variant first edition of a Wodehouse book. In those days of letterpress, when making up the prelims of the next book it was easy enough to take the prelims of the last book, adjust the first half-title, add a book title to the list of previous books by the author, adjust the title page, copyright page, and list of contents. But I missed the fact that the previous book *A Few Quick Ones* (1959) had had a second half-title inserted in order to spread the prelims. Unfortunately I overlooked this when making up the prelims of *Jeeves in the Offing* (1960). Hence copies of *Jeeves in the Offing* had a second half-title saying *A Few Quick Ones*. This was spotted early on, and the selling of the book was stopped and that page removed, and so there are just a small number of copies of the Leventhal variant out there.

The Herbert Jenkins building in Duke of York Street is still there, a narrow, nineteenth-century building with five floors. One evening I was working late writing copy for a promotion of books on the occult – wonderful, strong, atmospheric books on vampires and witchcraft by Montague Summers. Everybody had gone home when I heard a sound that caused me to look out of the window alongside my desk on the fourth floor. There was a white face looking in at me! In controlled haste, and certainly I would deny that there was any sense of panic, I rapidly descended the four floors and left the building. Which was when I realised that it had become dark whilst I was working, and the window had become mirror-like and the face at the window was my own reflection.

I enjoyed publishing so much that, being without commitments, I took a flat in town so as to be able to be in early and leave late without commuting to my family home in Edgware. In order to find a place within walking distance I placed a small ad in the London *Times*, saying that an impecunious young publisher needed a weekday *pied-à-terre*. I had several responses, and the one that I took up provided me with a penthouse in South Street, Mayfair. The owner was a Continental businessman who travelled a lot but had a young family. Although he had staff he wanted to know that there was someone else in the house at night-time. No duties went with this implied obligation. When we came to the amount for me to pay for the L-shaped penthouse, with views over the roofs of Mayfair, he asked me how much I could afford. I said £8 a week, and we made a deal. Using this apartment enabled me to walk to and from work, through Shepherd Market where I had breakfast with the taxi drivers, and along Piccadilly. Amongst the benefits of living in town was being able to go sometimes to the all-night trad jazz sessions at the 100 Club. I could leave at 5am or thereabouts, walk along Oxford Street, see milk being delivered, freshen up and be in the office early. That's one thing I couldn't do today. I guess it made me, in modern parlance, a clubber.

Publishing was so absorbing and so much fun (it was wonderful to get paid for such enjoyment) that on one occasion it was not until someone mentioned to me, with obvious relief, that the freighter had turned back that I even knew about the Cuban missile crisis. Because I was so fascinated with publishing I did take a little time out to research and write some articles, such as 'The Night the Book Trade Burned' about the blitz on London, and 'When They Tried to Tax Books' about purchase tax, and which appeared in *The Bookseller*.

A benefit of working in St. James's was being introduced to the London Library, just around the corner from the office. This wonderful establishment is one that no bookman could live without. Another was Fortnum & Mason, and being able to buy their fine fruit or flowers for special young ladies.

My affection for the London Library is such that I gave to them a small bequest of books that were left to me by an uncle. My mother's brother, Jack Woolf, was an artist, and his work was hung in the Summer Exhibition of the Royal Academy on more than one occasion. He tried to earn his living as an artist in the days when there was very little scope for this. His art was not of a commercial nature, and he was not a graphic designer, and he in fact ended up earning a living by restoring miniatures. During his lifetime he built a collection of art, which he bequeathed to me, but it was all of small items and nothing of significant value. Although he believed that he had some Rembrandt etchings, these turned out to be fakes when I had them expertly appraised and I was glad he never learned this. Other than the paintings by Jack himself, and a portrait of a lady by Maurice Greiffenhagen that hangs on the wall of the Greenhill offices, I sold off all the items of art at auction, but I felt that I just could not sell off his library of 200 or 300 prime books. Hence I gave them to the London Library, and in making the gift said that if there were any books that they did not wish to have it was not incumbent upon them to accept them all as part of a bequest, and they could feel free to dispose of them and possibly sell them to use the money to acquire books they needed. In the event they retained all the books, and I was exceedingly pleased when some years later I was researching a project for Lund Humphries and I found myself borrowing a book with my uncle's bookplate. I thought how pleased he would have been.

I was able to create a number of special launches for books, the directors at Herbert Jenkins pretty well giving me a free hand to do anything that sounded positive and didn't cost a great deal. When we published the show business memoirs of Ruby Miller entitled *Champagne from My Slipper* we held an autographing party at Hatchards. We arranged for a coach and horses to bring this old lady, who had until the 1920s been a major musical comedy star, along Piccadilly to the shop. It was a quiet news day and we achieved excellent television coverage (eleven times over four days), which caused the book to sell out. It was only after the book was on sale, and selling well, that a sharp-eyed reader telephoned to point out that this lady had already published the identical volume in the 1920s. Fortunately nobody else did.

Another special event was when we took over the swimming pool at the Shell building on London's South Bank to present a new American safety technique called 'drownproofing'. We brought in some Scouts from Wales who had tested the technique, and filled the area to capacity with about three hundred of those involved with the sporting and sports education world. We also had quite a number of television teams, much to the consternation of the management of the Shell building who had let us use their facilities without charge, for their own publicity purposes, and now the television trucks filled the car-parks and wires were run everywhere. Then, half an hour before the drownproofing presentation began, I saw a television team start to pack up. And then another. I hastened over and was told that Nehru had died, and that they were being despatched immediately to the Indian High Commission. All the television teams had pulled out by the time of the presentation, and we got no coverage at all in the general media, but the sporting education world was certainly most interested. I've never checked since then however as to whether drownproofing, as a method for survival at sea, became widely taught. But the book sold out.

I had started visiting the Frankfurt Book Fair in order to sell translation rights to books, and the book *Drownproofing* was one that I had bought for Jenkins when on a visit to publishers in New York. One book that we did not publish was about Maria Callas. I had found a small American publisher who had the rights to the book by her mother. It was somewhat shallow, and justified Callas's unhappy upbringing and early exploitation. We were not sure about libel, and when the diva was in London thought that the best way to check if she felt kindly towards the book was to ask her for a Foreword. A telephone call came from her, from her suite at the Savoy: 'My mother's story is all rather sad, and we would prefer it not to be published in Britain.' Yes, diva, we concurred.

It was at Jenkins that I started having lunchtime meetings, a publishing tradition that I have been only too happy to maintain over the years. The favourite place in those days was the then new Carvery at the Regent Palace Hotel, where a young man (who had no evening meal) could be wholly satisfied. More sophisticated was the Blue Post, which was a 'gentlemen only' dining room until the early 1980s. When they announced that ladies would be permitted I took Rosemary, my secretary, who usually made my lunchtime reservations there. She was the first lady to lunch there (although of course others were permitted to act as waitresses). A number of heads were turned (in fact quite naturally, because Rosemary was lovely) but negatively, and the management was called over to several tables to confirm that, heaven forfend, women were now permitted to lunch with gentlemen.

As my role with Herbert Jenkins evolved and I worked more and more on the promotion and sale of books, I took over as sales director. But as the non-fiction publishing programme grew successfully, and so too the sales, in 1964 Derek Grimsdick and family, the owners of Herbert Jenkins, sold the business to Barrie & Rockcliffe, and very shortly and painfully thereafter my services were no longer required. I had been told that I would be sales director of the two companies brought together, but was then instructed to give notice of dismissal to the Herbert Jenkins sales team. When I suggested that both teams should be assessed and the best of each maintained, this was not advice that was welcomed and so I left at the same time as my team. Herbert Jenkins had to evacuate the building at quite short notice, and we were instructed to dispose of as much as possible. An enormous amount of material had built up in the thirty or forty years that Herbert Jenkins had occupied the building, including masses of old manuscripts, artwork, etc. At that time there was no value put on manuscripts and artwork, but I bundled up those of P. G. Wodehouse, and his books, and sent them for safety to David Jasen in the United States.

The two companies, Herbert Jenkins and Barrie & Rockcliffe, amalgamated to become Barrie & Jenkins, and was eventually taken over by Hutchinson, who were taken over by Century, who were taken over by Random House (now owned by Bertels-mann). There are still a small number of books in print from my days, most notably Godden's *Encyclopedia of British Pottery and Porcelain Marks*, and when I see such I still regard them as 'my' books.

Looking back, I knew nothing about publishing when I joined Herbert Jenkins (except that it paid better than bookselling) but guess that I did things with a certain energy and have to say that I rather think that my approach, only in the interests of getting things done, may have required patience by the directors. After my departure, and unhappy time with Paul Hamlyn, I decided to try and publish on my own, and as I knew nothing of business methods and indeed there was no enterprise culture to learn from, I was often facing new and unfamiliar situations. Whenever I came to a bump on the ground, certainly if of a moral nature, I would try and envisage how Derek and Tom would have dealt with it. I would try and work out how I could explain a situation to them, and if I could then the answer would be clear to me.

3

THE START OF MY
MILITARY BOOK PUBLISHING

IT WAS WHILST I WAS AT HERBERT JENKINS that I started my involvement with military book publishing, in 1960, working on the
publication of my first book of military interest. Looking back
from a long career professionally concerned with books on military subjects, and with the benefit of hindsight, one can see a
distinct line for publishing on military subjects, but it wasn't
planned like that.

At Herbert Jenkins two of the developments were the undertaking of the distribution of US publishers' lists and the
publishing, not arranged by me but by a colleague, of some of
the best books about sports shooting. It was at that time that I
started working with the specialist bookseller Ken Trotman.
Jenkins could not advertise such books and offer them for sale
by mail; it was not the custom at the time for any publisher to
sell direct to the public. Hence we arranged advertisements
using Ken Trotman's name, and large spaces for books such as
Shotgun Marksmanship in magazines such as *Shooting Times*
brought dozens and dozens of orders. I worked on the US
imported books from Stackpole and DBI, but can't claim that
there was a master plan which led to my own military
publishing because I also worked on other books, most notably
on antique collecting and the occult (and of course one wishes
one could be prescient in forecasting sales). I had no understanding of sports shooting, but then we had contact with Major
E. G. B. Reynolds and that was something of a change of direction. Major Reynolds was working on a history of the Lee-Enfield
rifle; would we be interested in publishing it? The answer was
'yes'. Major Reynolds brought to the subject a particular knowledge, for he had managed the manufacture in World War II of

the then latest, and final, model of the firearm. We saw the book as appealing to collectors (and the Herbert Jenkins list had a number of books on collecting subjects which I was developing) and this was therefore seen as a 'fit', especially with the imported books on firearms. We had sales in the United States particularly in mind: the British Government had sold off four million surplus guns there for hunting. *The Lee-Enfield Rifle*, which had a distinctive jacket designed by me, was published on 18 March 1960, and if there has to be a starting date for my association with publishing on military subjects then that is it.

I was also fortunately correct about the interest in the United States, for we were able to sell a co-edition to Arco of New York.

I visited the Victoria and Albert Museum a number of times to make contacts for contributions to the new *Victorian Collector Series*, Jenkins being possibly the only publishing house at the time to show an interest in books on antiques, and the curator in charge of metalwork – Claude Blair – was enormously helpful. He put us in touch with Howard L. Blackmore and this led to his definitive *British Military Firearms 1650–1850* being published in April 1961 (and reissued by Greenhill Books in the 1990s). Howard Blackmore was with Customs & Excise, specialising in the diamond trade. He had spent two decades researching in the Ordnance records, and produced wholly new material about the history of British firearms, in a major work of reference which is a permanent, and unequalled, contribution to the subject area. Published simultaneously in 1961 with *British Military Firearms* was *Early Percussion Firearms* by Lewis Winant (bought in from an American publisher), and other books that followed included *A History of Spanish Firearms* by James Lavin. These led on to the *Arms & Armour Series*, which was commissioned before I left Jenkins, but published afterwards.

Another book on a military subject published at Herbert Jenkins was *Military Costume* by Paul Martin, a large-format work in colour, originated in Germany, which I found at the Frankfurt Book Fair (as *Der Bunte Rock*, released by Jenkins in a joint English/German-language edition), and when I left Jenkins for Hamlyn I arranged their cheap edition reprint which sold well for many years. Some might see a straight line between the 1963 book *Military Costume* and *Napoleon's Elite Cavalry* in 1999, of which more later.

It was at that time that I began my liaisons with authorities on the history of weapons, such as A. V. B. Norman (known to his friends as Nick) who was then with the Wallace Collection, H. Russell Robinson at the Royal Armouries, HM Tower of London, Frederick J. Wilkinson, W. Y. Carman and others. I could probably list several dozen books I have published over the years by them, and others they introduced me to, as one

Starting young: 'Ronnie the Rep', who comments on the book trade every week in Publishing News, *is Lionel Leventhal's favourite cartoon. Artist Mike Dickinson, a sales representative for enfant terrible Lionel Leventhal many years ago, kindly drew this cartoon especially for the thirtieth anniversary (1960–90) of his military publishing.*

project led to another. They all produced work which made a contribution to the subject area and has stood the test of time.

When I went to Hamlyn it was in a general role, and I had no plans to set up my own independent publishing. Hamlyn, however, was not for me, and things evolved, and it was as Arms & Armour Press that I started publishing military books on my own in 1966, based on the contacts made and relationships formed at Herbert Jenkins.

Many books that I have been involved with over the years have become collectors' items and fetch enhanced prices when they go out of print. For my first military books published at Herbert Jenkins the original published prices and approximate collectors' prices today are:

The Lee-Enfield Rifle: 42 shillings / now £65
British Military Firearms: 50 shillings / now £65
    notwithstanding the recent Greenhill revised reprint
Early Percussion Firearms: 50 shillings / now £30
History of Spanish Firearms: 63 shillings / now £45
Military Costume: 70 shillings / now £25

The continuing value of these books, a couple of which have been reprinted several times, is measured by their enhanced retail prices. Few enough books increase in price when they go out of print.

4

WITH PAUL HAMLYN

WHEN I LEFT JENKINS, precipitately and unhappily, word about this spread and I was approached by Philip Jarvis, one of the team of three who ran Hamlyn (the others being Paul himself, and Ralph Vernon Hunt), and I joined as Philip's PA. Language evolves over the years and in those days to be a PA meant 'deputy', even amanuensis, but nowadays it is often used for secretarial staff.

At that time, in 1964, Hamlyn was one of the most vigorous forces in the profession, doing exciting things and publishing wonderful and innovative books in colour. Paul was the creative genius, Ralph ran the best sales machine in Britain and Philip made things happen. They were the founders and dynamo behind a force that was changing the face of British publishing.

As I joined, Hamlyn was bought by IPC, the publisher of newspapers such as the *Daily Mirror*, and book imprints, in a sensational agreed take-over. Whilst I was there, Hamlyn was given the eleven loss-making other IPC book publishing companies, such as Newnes and Odhams, to run and integrate. With that act lay the seeds of destruction because it changed an entrepreneurial business with a wonderful *esprit de corps* into a corporate organisation.

The small, tight-knit management team went out for lunch each day and I joined this during my first week. Lunching is one of the pleasures of publishing, but at that time I had never had a business orientated lunch. I checked what sort of restaurant we would go to: Italian. I quaked; Italian restaurants were somewhat new to London, difficult as that is to believe nowadays, and I had never been to one. I hastened to the cookery book department for a briefing, and by the time we went out I knew what to order. This was shortly after a fast food place had opened close to the Herbert Jenkins offices that offered for the first time in Great Britain something entirely new, imported from Italy, and was a test to see if the British would enjoy Italian fast food. We were not even sure how to pronounce the name of the food – 'pizza'.

As I joined the Hamlyn offices moved from Fulham to Drury Lane. On one side of the building we could look into the men's dressing rooms of the famous Theatre Royal, and on the other the ladies' toilets of the adjacent offices. I telephoned the personnel manager of the other offices to explain the problem, and he questioned why the previous occupants of our new offices had never raised the matter.

We were on the edge of Covent Garden market, where parking restrictions did not apply, and if you drove up when the produce trucks were pulling out first thing in the morning, and appropriately tipped the gaffer in charge of truck parking, he could let you park for free all day.

Although I was ostensibly deputy to Philip Jarvis, it soon became apparent that he couldn't deputise (or maybe I couldn't be deputised to), and I didn't have a role nor could I play the necessary big firm politics. But suddenly there arose a severe problem for the management, and as I was the only spare body I was overnight transferred to the new company, Music for Pleasure. Music for Pleasure, called MfP, was the first mass market budget record label in Britain, and Paul had brought all the flair that he had in creating new book markets to the new enterprise. But little else. Everyone within Hamlyn had thought that everyone else was dealing with matters, and there was no-one in charge of many aspects of the new business. For example, as MfP was a joint company with EMI, each thought that the other was dealing with arrangements for royalties on the records, and neither had budgeted for any. I moved in to take charge of sales, and had to take radical action (a euphemism for asking some people to stay after 5.30pm and then having them clear their desks and depart). When the national launch took place 78 LPs were released simultaneously at 12s. 6d., and this was a sensation reported on television and in the press.

We then found that the national delivery system was in chaos, and nobody knew what shops had ordered what records, and where they were. Although there was a very simple invoicing system, with all the records listed on one side of a sheet, there was no accounting system and no way to access the information (and customers were screaming for delayed supplies, misdirected consignments and so forth). I sorted the matter out by arranging for the large, showpiece book showroom to be stripped empty during the night, and trestle tables and temporary workers to be there the next morning. Each table was given one or more letter of the alphabet, and the temps sorted for three days, fifteen hours a day, and then were able to keep the paper mountain under control. We had got things in order, but the showroom was the pride and joy of the powerful sales team at Hamlyn, and they were not happy bunnies.

When things settled down at MfP I was again a free hand, in senior management, and regarded as an object of suspicion by the staff, but with nothing to do. By that time the various IPC publishing companies were supposedly to be brought together, and I was put on the small planning team. Paul wanted to know nothing about it.

There were two aspects to the integration: the command by IPC to have all their book publishing businesses, which were spread over a multiplicity of buildings, brought together into a single space, and deciding whether in bringing companies together and amalgamating functions everyone would be wanted.

There were at that time in the London area only about four or five buildings available that could house the number of staff there were, or were going to be. All were in frankly unsuitable locations, but I decided that the one at Feltham was the best, especially because it was well positioned for Heathrow Airport. On one of my visits I took with me a camera and I lay down on the green two or three hundred yards away facing the centre at Feltham and took a series of photographs, which made the building look handsome and placed in a parkland. These were presented to Paul who agreed to the renting of the building, but swore that he would never use it himself. It was, in fact, after the signing for the building that I decided that there was no future for me with the company and planned my departure (which took place before the announcement of the move to the staff). In the event, Hamlyn were only in the building for about two years. During that time some of the problems of consolidation came home to roost, and for the first time ever the Hamlyn business made a loss. A massive loss. However, because we had acquired what had been an empty whole building we had negotiated an extremely advantageous long-term rent, and putting the building on the market with the original fixed rent produced a magnificent benefit.

The other aspect of integrating the companies was staff reduction, and in one meeting with Philip Jarvis we produced a listing of names of people who were going to be encouraged, one way or another, to pursue their careers elsewhere (although there was not all that much we could do directly about it due to watertight union restrictions). It was over the next two years that some wonderfully talented people who had helped the growth of Hamlyn left, and it seemed that everyone on our list was promoted. All those whom we had thought we would be best without were in positions of senior management. The losses continued.

One aspect of being part of a newspaper conglomerate was that the staff had to join the appropriate trade union, for those were the days of closed shops and very severely restrictive practices. At the drop of a hat they would stop, or threaten to stop, production of the *Daily Mirror*. Union holders had ranking titles, and each local unit was called a 'Chapel'. The person in charge of the Chapel was called the 'Father', and I didn't know this and was somewhat bemused on first being told that the Father of Chapel wanted to meet with me. There was a progression to this, and when the person to whom all the Chapels reported wanted to meet with me I found it difficult to contain myself when I was told that the Imperial Father was coming to my office. But such became serious business, and nothing to do with publishing but politics and power, which was a game that I could not play.

My office at Hamlyn was off another, off a large open-plan floor. One day as the telephone rang I noticed through the partition windows that people seemed to be heading towards the exit door. The caller was a girl I knew and was distancing myself from, and maybe I had not been specific but she certainly wasn't receiving the signals. 'Hello Lionel, I'm glad that at last I've got you. We need to talk,' she said. It was then that I noticed the smoke; the building was obviously being evacuated but nobody (later I wondered why) had thought of me in my office off another. 'I'm sorry, but I can't talk now; I have to dash – it looks as though the building is on fire,' I replied. She was vehement, as I saw the clouds of smoke start to billow: 'You keep giving me excuses as to why we can't talk; if you don't make time for me now we are finished.' It was obviously a time for making a decision, one of life's turning points. I put the telephone down, and ran through the smoke to the exit. It only took a short time to ascertain that the fire that caused so much smoke to billow through the air conditioning outlets was of no consequence, but I was free again.

Without a role, as something of a political non-person, I took a break, a touring holiday in the Cotswolds, to think about things, and whilst listening to the Mamas and Papas sing about *California Dreaming* on the car radio determined to leave although I did not have a job to go to. I agreed my departure and when I left Hamlyn was quoted in the trade press that 'I wanted to return to publishing', and this did not help me win friends or influence people there.

Paul Hamlyn became a very wealthy man, was ennobled, and endowed a Foundation. Today the Foundation sponsors, probably amongst other things, education in publishing, and I have been very happy to take advantage of it for members of my team.

5

ARMS & ARMOUR PRESS:
GETTING STARTED

THERE WERE THREE DISTINCT STAGES to the evolution of Arms & Armour Press, each different in time-span but with significant differences in the development of the publishing house: working from home, 1966–69; first offices in Childs Hill, North West London, 1969–71; and the offices in Hampstead High Street, 1971–84.

At the time that I left Paul Hamlyn to start Arms & Armour Press publishing houses were eponymous and publishing books of a general nature; British publishing in the mid-1960s was not forward-looking and almost no new publishing houses were being set up.

Hence I called the new business Arms & Armour Press because I did not want my own name upon it in case it failed, or (preferably) I received a job offer. A plus factor, however, was that it neatly covered and advertised the subject area upon which I proposed to publish, and over a period as the publishing developed, this attracted attention, and made it a sympathetic name in the subject area. There have been few enough subject specific publishing houses, and there was none of such a nature at that time.

Doing business with three people whom I knew from my Herbert Jenkins days was what established Arms & Armour Press. These were Ken Trotman, the specialist military bookseller, Milton Gladstone, an avuncular pirate of a publisher running Arco in New York, and Nat Wartels of Crown, New York. Also I must mention Charles Letts, the very long-established diary publishers, with whom I acted as a consultant for their getting into book publishing, and this generated a positive personal cash flow.

The way into doing business without delay was to reissue sought-after books. I have noticed businesses set up and create overheads and then wait for new books to be written and published, which can build an edifice of debt. I didn't have that time, and I had no money or financial backing. I was fortunate to be personally without commitments, and to live and be able to work from my parents' house in Edgware, Middlesex, on the edge of London's north-western suburbs. I set up a desk in my bedroom, and had a telephone line extension. My mother would answer downstairs and then put through telephone calls, sometimes international ones which were a rare occurrence in those days, to her son 'Mr Leventhal' – in my bedroom. Books were packed for despatch on the kitchen table. Another time, inspectors from the Government's Export Credit Guarantee Department made a visit, and were slightly astonished to have to have a meeting in the dining room of a residential house in the suburbs with a new business which was exporting books (in bulk, directly from printers) to the United States.

The first books to be reprinted were very modest, but were undertaken at the behest of Ken Trotman. They were reprints, in stiff paper covers, of nineteenth-century military source material, such as *Military Breech-Loading Small Arms* by V. D. Majendie (1868), and *Early Breech-Loaders* by John Latham (1867). The quantity being reprinted was only 300 copies, but Ken Trotman had guaranteed to take 100 of each and that sale funded the whole print run.

There are all sorts of comparisons that can be made between the enterprise culture that was created in the 1970s and subsequently took off in the 1980s, and the professionalism in business today. Back in the 1960s such a culture did not exist, there was no guidance or education, and if one realised just how much one didn't know one would not have commenced business, at all. However the business world was also much simpler. It seemed to me to be a practical situation (whilst still looking for a job), that if one could sell sufficient books to pay the printer's bill and get the payment from the customer before the printer's bill was due for payment then everything would add up. It has always focused the mind wonderfully when the monies you are spending must come from your own (possibly empty) pocket.

The first thing to do for the first publication was to research and locate a firm that could economically print a quantity as low as 300 copies. As those were the days of folk music, I checked the shelves of some Charing Cross Road bookshops, and a few coffee shops, for the name of any firm which printed the short runs of folk music fanzines. I found a printer working from a shed by a creek in Essex, and it was that printer who produced the first Arms & Armour Press books. I would pick the stock up from his shed and drive with them over to High Wycombe and deliver them, with the invoice, to Ken Trotman.

Parallel to this I started clearing copyrights on full-scale books which Ken Trotman said were wanted by the gun collectors. He, however, could not take more than a guaranteed 100 out of the possible print run of between 1,500 and 2,500, which was needed in order to sell at a realistic retail price. Hence using the contacts that I had made through visiting New York and selling co-editions for Herbert Jenkins I got in touch with Milton Gladstone and Nat Wartels. Both were happy to take co-editions of books such as *English, Irish and Scottish Firearms Makers* by A. Merwyn Carey, *Sword, Lance and Bayonet* by Charles ffoulkes, *British Pistols and Guns* by Ian Glendenning, etc. Nat Wartels took an especially large quantity of *The Gun and its Development* by W. W. Greener: 8,000 copies of this monster 852-page book for 12s. 7d. each. Maybe indeed it's now time for another reprinting.

Milton was short, avuncular and cigar-chewing; an archetypal New York wheeler and dealer. He always claimed that Milo Minderbinder who wheeled and dealed his way through World

War II in the book *Catch-22* was based on him, and Minderbinder certainly reflected his way of doing business.

Nat Wartels had a unique office, and his desk was piled high with a mountain of papers three or four feet high. In fact as you went into his office you could not see him at all, and had to go round the side of his desk. He, however, knew unerringly where every sheet of paper he needed was, and could reach into a higgledy-piggledy heap of paper and bring it out. He continued for many years his active publishing work, indeed his personal ownership of Crown, until he was well into his eighties. Then he sold the business, although he stayed on. But as these things happen, it just wasn't the same. The new owners cleared his desk, and it felt wrong seeing him across a gleaming, clear space.

These co-edition orders from American publishers, as with the low run reprints, enabled the printers' bills for the whole editions to be paid and, if my judgement was right, there would be profit from the sale of the remaining copies of the books which I had kept for Arms & Armour Press's own publication.

The first and modest facsimile publications came out as I was leaving Paul Hamlyn, in October 1966. There were eight more publications in 1967, three of them in hardback that were sold on a co-edition basis to Arco. Ten more books followed in 1968, which is when I started working again with Stackpole Books, on a co-edition basis, with the *Arms & Armour Press Illustrated Monographs*.

Whilst still working from home in 1968 there was, with the benefit of hindsight, one significant trendsetting publication: that of *The Sherman* by Peter Chamberlain and Chris Ellis. This was only a modest, illustrated paperback, but it led on to major works such as *British and American Tanks of World War II* and *Tanks of the World* by the same authors, *German Tanks of World War II* by von Senger und Etterlin, and *Russian Tanks 1900–1970* by John Milsom. They were the first of a whole generation of 'nuts and bolts' books.

The publication of books for collectors led to our exhibiting at the newly established London Arms Fair, where we could sell the reprints of source works about firearms. At one Fair the purchaser of a costly, antique bayonet came over to the Arms & Armour Press stand to check the new book *Bayonets* by F. J. Stephens, in order to identify the specific model that he had just spent a lot of money upon. He found a photograph of his bayonet in it, but then dithered about paying £1.50 for the book. He spent much time moaning about the high cost of books, especially when all he wanted was just the one page, and when he eventually, reluctantly, made up his mind to buy it I refused to sell him a copy. Fortunately a friend of his came over ten minutes later to buy the book for him; I needed every sale I could get.

The publication of the book *Rapiers* by Eric Valentine almost led to a dreadful embarrassment. Publishers often turn to experts for a critical opinion of material that is being submitted to them, and this is a practice that I have always followed, starting at Arms & Armour Press and continuing to this day. In order to have the expert express a factual, critical opinion, the publisher must offer confidentiality (unless the expert says that his name can be revealed), because often the expert may have to work with in some way, or may even be a friend of, the author whose material is being submitted. In this particular case Eric Valentine was a wonderful, larger than life, ebullient Mancunian, who collected with great gusto, but his knowledge was not academically based. A. V. B. Norman, then Deputy Director of the Wallace Collection, was the great expert on the subject, with a wonderful dry wit, and he wrote a report that said that only the photographs of the swords from the book were of any value; the text was worthless. He called me and made me promise on my honour that his friend Eric would not know it was he who had given the opinion, and I agreed. I wrote letters to both A. V. B. Norman and Eric Valentine, and it was only when I was on the way to the post-box that something made me pause, open one of the letters, and – yes – the letters had been switched in the envelopes. It certainly would have been hideously embarrassing to all concerned if the wrong letter had been sent to Eric Valentine.

The address used on the first Arms & Armour Press books was that of my home in Edgware, but this soon changed when Clive Bingley, then running his publishing business of professional books for librarians, undertook the trade distribution, and the address changed to his base in Pembridge Road, Notting Hill, until we moved into our first offices.

With the evolution and growth of the publishing it became necessary to have offices, and I decided to have them in North West London, convenient for a journey from home and for visitors from Central London. Also, a major step for any new business, I decided to take on an employee.

6

ARMS & ARMOUR PRESS:
THE FIRST OFFICES

IN THE SUMMER OF 1969 I moved into the first Arms & Armour Press offices, a small, historic building, on Finchley Road, in Childs Hill, North West London. We were in these offices for under three years, but they were pivotal to the growth of the publishing house.

David Gibbons, one of the first full-time employees at Arms & Armour Press, joined the firm, followed by John Walter and Anthony Simmonds. David Gibbons became a director a few years later, and after I sold Arms & Armour Press he departed to set up his own book production and design unit and our association, together with Tony Evans, who also worked for Arms & Armour Press, continues. John Walter left after a few years, but undertook the authorship of a number of important books on guns for both Arms & Armour Press and, subsequently, Greenhill Books, and again the association continues. When Anthony Simmonds left it was to enter bookselling, and eventually he set up his own business and is today a leading dealer in naval books and, of course, a Greenhill Books customer. Hence there is a continuing relationship in place, for more than thirty years, with four of the team from the early days of Arms & Armour Press.

In that summer of 1969 man landed on the moon, live on television (prime time in the United States, but early in the morning in Britain). In the Finchley Road offices the publishing programme also took a giant leap forward: significant books were then being published such as *German Tanks of World War II* by von Senger und Etterlin, *British and American Tanks of World War II* by Peter Chamberlain and Chris Ellis, *British Smooth Bore Artillery* by Major General B. P. Hughes, *Badges of the British Army* by Frederick J. Wilkinson, *Russian Tanks 1900-1970* by John Milsom and *Japanese Arms & Armour* by H. Russell Robinson (and some of these and other books produced at that time continue to be in print, regularly reprinted). The formula for publishing was very simple: if an American co-edition publisher would take a sufficient quantity, at a price which would fund the publication of the book, then not only would one proceed with that but one would look for another follow-up project, which could also be sold to that publisher. One would run like hell to meet the delivery date that had been agreed before any production work had in fact been commenced (or money spent on the book). We lived within the printer's period of credit.

The authors of most of these books had a museum connection. The translation of *German Tanks of World War II* from the German was by James Lucas, then with the Imperial War Museum. This was his first writing project and led to a long authorship career. *British Smooth Bore Artillery* was by the remarkable 'Bil' Hughes, a gunner, and I visited him at the Royal Artillery Institution in Woolwich. He also wrote *Firepower*, a fine work. *German Army Uniforms and Insignia* was the first of several works on German uniforms of World War II by Brian L. Davis, who acted as a consultant on films such as *Where Eagles Dare*. H. Russell Robinson was with the Royal Armouries, at the Tower of London, and later wrote the much valued *Armour of Imperial Rome*. I would visit with him at the Tower of London, and in those terrorist-free days, and if one had permission, one could drive past the entrance where visitors paid to go into the Tower, down a few yards to the Embankment between the Tower and the Thames, and along it to the far end of the Tower where there was a bridge and a gateway for permitted visitors to drive in, and park outside the Royal Armouries. It was a privilege to be allowed to do so, and traffic was rare. One day when the Embankment area was full of tourists, and I was driving extremely slowly so that those visiting the Tower had time to get out of the way, one tourist started to wave and clap, so I waved back. So as the crowd parted to allow me passage they were all waving and clapping. I could but wave, and wonder who on earth they thought they were seeing. Then, fortunately, I reached the bridge into the Tower itself, and was able to get away from the crowd.

It was at this time that the distinctive A&AP logo was designed, and the clear and simple initials appeared on a great many books over the years.

With the development of Arms & Armour Press we set to one side the publishing of books on automobiles, although we published eight titles in a special landscape format under the Lionel Leventhal Limited imprint. If they had been more successful I might now have been writing about a career publishing motoring literature.

There can often be interesting problems when it comes to clearing copyrights, and getting permission to reprint books. When we wanted to reprint a security restricted official military manual from the end of World War II entitled *Red Army Uniforms, 1944*, I made the appropriate enquiry for copyright clearance, and the message came back that the work did not exist. I gently pointed out that I was holding a copy, but this couldn't be accepted because on the one hand the work did not exist and on the other hand as it was security restricted it could not be held by a lay-person. Official permission could not be given until the work had been inspected, and officialdom didn't have a copy. I was advised to let them have my copy, but I suddenly got queasy in case when I handed it over a handcuff would be clapped onto my wrist, or if it was still restricted I then could not have it back. A hand-over arrangement was agreed, which would leave me free, and which would enable the book to come back to me. All of this was nearly twenty-five years after the end of the war, and our whole reason for wanting to undertake the reprint was the interest in the historic uniforms worn by the Soviets at the end of World War II. Finally, yes, we were given permission and I did get the book back.

To clear the copyright on another early publication of Arms & Armour Press I was searching for information about the author, and one of our contacts told us that there was a plaque giving his date of death in a church in a little village on the Isle of Wight. In Britain one has to find the date of death in order to obtain the person's will, to see to whom he would have willed his literary estate (there's no central repository of copyright information, as there is in the United States). The problem was how to obtain the information from the plaque? It was a very small village, and there was no librarian I could telephone, and so I telephoned the local general store. When I asked them to go over the road and check in the churchyard I rather think that they thought I was someone from the television programme *Candid Camera*. They said that I should telephone back later on in the day, and when they were less busy. They then were, in fact, very helpful and provided the information which enabled us to trace the will and enabled a reprinting to be undertaken.

Whilst in the Finchley Road offices I met with a number of authors with whom long relationships began. One significant author was Ian V. Hogg, and I met with him when he was thinking of retiring from the armed services and starting a career as a writer. He was a Master Gunner in the Royal Artillery, and obviously very knowledgeable indeed. The major question, however, when he visited was whether, notwithstanding his knowledge, he could write and communicate it and present material in a professional fashion and on schedule. We had lots of ideas for new reference books on weapons, but started him with a small, containable project. This was his *Military Pistols and Revolvers*, his first firearms book which was published in 1970. Yes, the book was indeed ideal, was successful, and was the founding book of his many books on military equipment. To help decorate my new offices he kindly provided a rifle for a display panel. I then received an urgent telephone call a few days later: 'Hide that rifle! I have to take it away.' I'm not sure what the problem was but within hours he appeared and the rifle disappeared.

Ian Hogg was one of only fourteen Master Gunners in the British Army, there being in fact fewer Master Gunners than Field Marshals. On one of his visits to the office he came in uniform: khaki with Sam Browne belt and peaked cap, and rank badges on the cuff of the Royal Arms surrounded by a laurel wreath with a gun badge beneath. He had come by bus and told me how he had become conscious of an elderly gentleman across the aisle eyeing him up and down. As he stood to leave the bus the gentleman tugged at his sleeve. 'Excuse me,' he said, 'but are you a Master Gunner?' 'Yes I am,' Ian replied. 'Goodness me,' he exclaimed, 'I served twenty-eight years in the Gunners and you are the first one I've ever seen, and I do so here on a bus on the Finchley Road!'

Ian Hogg went on from *Military Pistols and Revolvers* to enjoy a long and continuing writing career, and has published to date over 150 books on military subjects.

I got to know the petrol station opposite the office, having an account and filling up there regularly. This stood me in good stead a few years later during the 'gas crunch' for I was able to phone the garage, make an appointment, and at the agreed time they would move the barrier and I could drive in for petrol.

I moved from being single, which had enabled me to work from my bedroom in my parents' home, to marrying my wife, Elizabeth, during this period. With the lead-in times required in publishing, there were sometimes quiet periods, and my wife's parents could not understand how when we were engaged in the late 1960s I was free to meet Elizabeth from the train near her home in the afternoons when she came home from work, and take her out swimming. Especially as at that time I had little enough visible means of support, and in those early days the publications were sixty-four-page A5 booklets. We honeymooned in Tenerife, with our plane having snow swept off the wings after a record February snowfall, were bumped from our hotel, and ended up staying in the hacienda of the mayor. But that's another story.

Early in 1971 I published my first book on the Napoleonic Wars. This was a reissue of Charles Dalton's *Waterloo Roll Call* (carefully reprinting the second edition, for this was a case when a second edition of a book contained revisions and was more valuable than the first edition). This was a first in another respect, being priced in the new decimal currency, following currency conversion from the historic 'pounds, shillings and pence'.

Sometime in 1970 I was driving up Hampstead High Street and saw an open space where builders had cleared a plot of land. There was just a hole in the ground as foundations were being excavated. I stopped, found the manager of the building works, and through him got in touch with lawyers and the property developer. There was little enough office space at that time in Hampstead and, indeed, little enough demand for such, so I was able to sign an advantageous lease before the building was above the ground. Hence Arms & Armour Press moved from Childs Hill to Hampstead in 1971, expanding into a newly built, large office space.

It is always a great temptation to undertake a project out of one's core publishing area and I succumbed to this, fortunately successfully, when we moved into Hampstead. To celebrate the move I published under the Lionel Leventhal Limited imprint a reprint of the classic, monumental *Annals of Hampstead* by Thomas J. Barrett.

To promote the work a four-page prospectus was produced, enveloped, and teams of newspaper boys distributed it on a door-to-door basis over a weekend around all the best areas in Hampstead. There was an immediate response – the police were called. At the time there was heightened tension in London due to an Arab terrorist campaign against Jews, and there is a significant Jewish population in Hampstead. The police had issued an announcement warning householders against unfamiliar envelopes coming through their letter boxes, especially if they had a raised strip. Yes, that's right: our friendly, brown manila envelope had a raised strip.

On Monday morning there was a message in the office for me to call the local police, who told me about the panic I had caused locally, and how a bomb squad had been called out to deal with the problem until they realised just what was happening. In addition to this, however, our own letter box was full with lots of orders, and *Annals of Hampstead* soon sold out and our reprint edition has become a collector's piece.

A couple of years later my wife and I undertook the publication from our home of *Elstree and Borehamwood Through Two Thousand Years* by Anthony Frewin, and a much slimmer book was produced, announced by means of the distribution of leaflets door to door, and quickly sold out.

7

'HELLO, ENGLISH'

THE MAJOR FOCAL TRADING POINT of the international book trade is the annual fair in Frankfurt.

My first visit to the Frankfurt Book Fair was in 1959, on behalf of Herbert Jenkins. I've been credited with having attended the first German Book Fair, but as this took place in the fifteenth century I have to say that it was just a little before my time.

Frankfurt was a very different city in 1959, still with evidence of the ravages of World War II. I stayed in a small hotel by the station, and received a very favourable impression of the friendly nature of German girls who greeted me warmly with 'hello, English' every time I went in or out of the hotel. I believe that my stay there was in fact the first time that the hotel had ever let a room for the whole night. I was, of course, entirely immersed in the world of the book.

A note-book I have from about that time shows that the exchange rate was DM11.50 to £1, and the total expenses for my trip, including the plane fare, were £41. 11s. 9d. The note-book also shows meetings with publishers with whom relationships were started that lasted over many, many years, some to this day, such as with the German military publishers Bernard & Graefe, and Motorbuch Verlag.

In those days the Book Fair fitted into the single, white-pillared building that is currently by the entrance gates, I believe nowadays used as an admissions hall. Beyond it was a string of about a dozen World War II Nissen huts, used for publishers' exhibits. All around, as far as the eye could see and over the entire site which is now covered with exhibition halls, including the residential blocks at the far end of the current area of the Frankfurt Book Fair, was clear and covered with black clinkers, the result of the bombing raids by the Allies in World War II on the adjacent Frankfurt railway marshalling yards.

My recollection of those days is that it was always raining. One moved from hut to hut through canvas tunnels, with duckboards underneath that squelched into the mud. The rain blew against the canvas of the tunnels, and it always seemed to be damp and chilly. There was a heavy metal door that had to be pushed open to go into the campus tunnel, and if the wind caught it, it would slam shut. I saw this happen and the reverberations knocked down the Faber stand, which was alongside the doorway. 'That's the third time it has happened,' exclaimed an exasperated sales manager. A few years later the Fair moved into the first new-generation building, the high-ceilinged 'Halle Funf', and this was extremely welcome. The car park was across the cinders, and one always seemed to have to dash from the heated hall through hard driven, cold rain to get to the car.

The 1960s saw a series of student demonstrations and riots, sometimes with running fights in the streets of Frankfurt, the Fair grounds and even in the halls themselves. Eventually the authorities regulated the students who agreed to demonstrate only at certain times, those being the times and places where television cameras were. It became 'demonstration for television camera', and it was either this or the lack of passion for some of the events that the students were demonstrating for which saw a decline in protests. The demonstrations over the years ranged from protesting against apartheid in South Africa to protesting even against the winner of the German book trade's Peace Prize; he was a very distinguished and cultured African, but his country had managed to upset somebody. One time I was in a taxi in downtown Frankfurt and we found a mass of students totally blocking the road. I had a tight schedule and was on the way to the airport, so the taxi driver shouted a curse at them, and drove straight through the crowd with bodies banging alongside and hurled off by the taxi. It was in those days that the stand for the Israeli publishers had to be surrounded by guards armed with sub-machine guns.

In one of those early days I do not believe that the sales manager I had with me had ever been abroad before, or if he had, he had not encountered a duvet. Over breakfast I asked if he had slept well, but unfortunately he had not. It turned out that he had been very uncomfortable, having unbuttoned the duvet and tried to sleep between the covers and the quilt.

In my first years of attending the Frankfurt Book Fair I stayed in small hotels in Frankfurt, and walked around the Fair visiting publishers rather than having a stand. As soon as Arms & Armour Press was established in the mid-1960s we had an exhibit, which meant having a car go to Frankfurt with books to display. Going by car meant being able to take one's books, but necessitated obtaining a carnet. Although books were not taxed, it was necessary to make a negative declaration. This meant having a document that detailed every book, which was a remarkably exacting typing job, because no errors were permitted, and it had to be done in six copies. There was only a very small amount of space in which to describe every title, even down to its weight, which was being taken over to the Frankfurt Book Fair and brought back, placing a deposit with the Chamber of Commerce as a guarantee that everything that went out would indeed come back. In addition it was absolutely essential as one passed each customs point going out of one country and into the next, to get that customs authority to place their stamp onto the documentation. Sometimes this entailed long delays. This occasionally involved stopping in some customs depot in the middle of the night. Sometimes it was only when one reached the next customs depot that one realised that one had not secured the appropriate exit stamp from the last depot, and it was necessary to go back. This never happened to my team, but we heard of people being turned back from entrance into France, because they hadn't received the correct British stamp of exit as they went onto a ferry, and having to shuttle back across the Channel to get the documentation stamped. The customs officials were mostly uninterested in books, and there was no inspection which was good because the order of the books listed on the carnet was not matched by the positioning of the books in the cartons.

One time on the journey home, however, having driven hard from a lunchtime close-down (which is sometimes described as being similar to the start of the Le Mans 24-hour race) at the Fair, across Germany and then Belgium, to a very late ferry and arriving even later in Britain, an extremely tired driver of the company car was told, very late at night (or perhaps early morning), that the British customs officer wanted to check the contents. He had to agree, but possibly the customs officer was also tired. He stood at the front of the vehicle calling out titles from the carnet, and our man stood at the back, in the dark, holding up books the wrong way round and saying 'yes, it's here'. The time that we certainly got the attention of a German customs officer was when in the typing of a couple of book titles they had been shortened from four copies of *The Book of Automatic Rifles*, etc., to '4 Automatic Rifles'.

Having a car also freed me from staying in Frankfurt and I explored the environs and discovered the little village of Kron-berg, in the Taunus mountains. This is a historic village, and my team and I have stayed ever since in one of its small hotels. Over the years, as hotels have closed or been refurbished, we have had to find alternative accommodation, but we are firmly established there, and indeed have had the pleasure of a number of overseas friends of ours staying with us. The advan-tage of Kronberg is that although one is staying in a fairly simple establishment, it is a pleasure to walk around the little village, and every night we can walk out to a different fine restaurant. Kronberg seems to have a dozen or so top quality restaurants, and we believe in having an early but long, leisurely, and most enjoyable dinner together, with guests. If the guests do not have their own transportation they are instructed to report to our stand at 6.25pm promptly; we can then close down the stand, lock away the dummies, go straight to the car park and leave the fairground. If all goes well we can be back in Kronberg, to the peace and quiet, for 7pm or shortly thereafter. We are then able to quickly freshen up, possibly have a drink, and then be seated at a restaurant and ordering food before 7.30pm. We've heard of some people who have to wait until well into the evening in downtown Frankfurt before being able to eat; that's not for me.

There have been many memorable dinners. One, a long time back, was when Peter Kindersley and I were seated together at a large dinner at the famous Buckenkeller in Frankfurt. He asked whether Dorling Kindersley should move from packaging into book publishing, thus building their own list. I advised 'What do you need all that trouble for? Why make all that additional investment, and take the risk? And of course you then have all the responsibilities for sales, marketing, distribution and so forth.' Needless to say he didn't accept this dinner-time advice.

A more recent problem is the new German public holiday to celebrate the reunification. We discovered the hard way that car parks are locked on public holidays; we had left our car overnight and could not gain access the following morning, which was the day of the holiday. Everywhere surrounding us was closed and there was no sign of life. Finally we saw a car using a special pass to enter the car park and we hurled ourselves in the style of Indiana Jones under the descending shutters and into the car park. We were fortunate in finding that in order to drive out there was an automatic exit button to push.

In fact I haven't been into downtown Frankfurt for possibly twenty years, and when the international publishers were exhibiting in Hall 4 and one could drive the car on to the roof-top car park and go down to the second floor of the hall where one's stand was, there was possibly a period of a number of years when my feet did not even touch the ground of Frankfurt.

1984 was a special Fair, for the documents to sell Arms & Armour Press were signed by me late on the afternoon of the day before I travelled to Germany. We had agreed a news black-out until I could tell the news personally to the members of the team who had gone ahead, which I had to do as I came off the plane and was collected by them. Thereafter news circulated with fascinating, remarkable speed. The editor of *The Bookseller* was however not happy, for he was trying to go to press early, from Germany, with the issue of the magazine which would be circulated at Frankfurt on that Saturday. We had a remarkable scramble to get in the story of the sale of Arms & Armour Press to Link House (which included Blandford, and which led a number of people to think that it was Blandford themselves who had taken over Arms & Armour Press), and I was surprised at the reaction it caused. All sorts of members of the trade came to see me, usually with kind messages, and a couple even claimed to have known for months that the deal was in progress, well before it had even been thought of or started.

The following year a similar situation occurred. My London Book Fair partner Clive Bingley and I took over Lund Humphries Publishers. Again the transaction took place the day before I travelled to the Fair. Again I thought that it was an important deadline due to the long lead-in time discussions about projects at the Fair with one's overseas colleagues and associates, and one needed to know where one stood in having such discussions. This time the news about the take-over circulated ahead of me and when I eventually arrived at the Frankfurt stand to help set it up there was an urgent – but urgent! – message to see

the editor of *The Bookseller*. He was extremely anxious to get the story into that week's magazine, and, from his viewpoint, we were making deals at the worst possible time in his scheduling.

Anecdotes about the Frankfurt Book Fair abound, but most are centred on specific projects that one happens to be working upon at the time, and the comradeship of meeting friends in the trade year after year. Sometimes it seems as though one picks up conversations uninterrupted from one year to the next.

Three Fairs – 1989, 1990 and 1991 – were especially memorable because of business with the Moscow publishing house, Planeta. The 1989 Fair saw the start of what became the sensationally successful book *Soviet Wings*. The next Frankfurt saw the book ready for co-edition publication, where we achieved in a few hectic days what might have taken months if we had had to send things by mail (in the days before courier or communication by computer). The book was published for the 1991 Fair, and we planned a celebratory dinner, held in Kronberg, and I invited an American publisher who had some knowledge of Russian and also a specialist interest in intelligence. This was that gentleman's first-ever Frankfurt Book Fair, and as he was an 'upfront' guy he mentioned at the start of the dinner that his Russian was a little rusty, but the last time he had heard it was when he was in Berlin and American intelligence had succeeded in tapping the Russian military telephone lines and he was one of the listeners. This was not a diplomatic thing to say, especially as the then Russian commercial structure was obviously part of the Soviet apparatus, and the fact that we were able to get the remarkable material that made *Soviet Wings* meant that we were dealing with people who either had a history somewhere in Soviet power, and who probably still had significant connections, or who were still involved. The temperature at the dinner table dropped. It dropped well below zero. The Soviet team leader exploded, and started shouting at us. His interpreter stopped translating. There was a period of embarrassment before we could change the conversation, unfortunately cutting our American friend out of it, and a subdued dinner ensued. By the end of it, following the consumption of much excellent German beer, a form of normality was in place and we parted with bear hugs.

I think that fewer deals are made nowadays, on the spot at any rate. Possibly this is because the Fair is only one, although very important, part of ongoing liaison with those with whom one does business. Or maybe the nature of my publishing has changed along with that of the overseas associates with whom we collaborate. I certainly recall far more deals being made on the spot yesteryear than today. One major transaction, made with a handshake, was at the 1973 Fair when I displayed the dummy of a large-format, colour book entitled *Butterflies of the World*. I had conceived the idea of bringing co-edition, colour techniques to works of reference, and in addition to being a beautiful volume it was scientifically valid, based upon the unique Natural History Museum collection in South Kensington, and showed 5,000 specimens. An American publisher seeing the dummy and reading the specification committed to a $100,000 purchase and in fact this led to a single, very large co-edition also being taken, for simultaneous printing, for publishers in Germany, Spain, France, Japan and I recall a couple of other countries. In the event, nothing that was in the dummy, the pages or its cover, was part of the finished and very successful book. But that's Frankfurt. Another made-on-the-spot deal was in 1976 with a new packager, Sidney Mayer, a somewhat larger than life American who had recently set up Bison Books in London. He had prepared *The Encyclopaedia of Infantry Weapons of World War II* by Ian V. Hogg. The book was a natural 'fit' with my Arms & Armour Press, and we both saw the natural price point at £4.95 (those were the days!). Working on the mark-up formula that I needed, I pressed for a reduction of a halfpenny. But Sid couldn't agree. There was an impasse, and it looked a though the deal might fall through. Doing some lateral thinking, and considering his somewhat piratical way of doing business, I suggested 'Let's toss for it.' We did, and I'm glad to say that I won. It was only afterwards that it was pointed out that I had tossed a coin for £45, something that I would never conceive of doing in the real world. I cannot recall deals like these in recent years, just solid and continuing relationships.

At and around the Fair there are parties of every shape, style and size. They are held on stands at the Fair, or at hotels and restaurants. We have had a number of parties on the stand over the years, a memorable recent one being a special celebration for the seventieth birthday of Edward Coffey from Australia, which had taken months to plan, and which brought together his friends and colleagues from Australia and New Zealand, Great Britain and the United States. A reception I especially remember was hosted by Bill Hanna, a Canadian publishing friend. This was to be held at his stand, and I went over and joined the crowd, nodded to several folk I met, and admired and much enjoyed the wonderful canapés and good wine that they were offering. When I looked around for my host however, to compliment him on the marvellous and generous spread, I became aware that neither he nor any of his colleagues were there. After a little pause, to enjoy another scrumptious canapé, I realised that I was at the wrong event. The event to which I had been invited was further down the same gangway at the Fair, and I duly had to make my excuses and move on. They were providing standard Fair edibles, but fortunately I had already eaten.

A French publisher once visited our stand with some handsome books, full of glorious paintings of battles. He could only speak French, and as an aside I asked one of my marketing colleagues, 'How come the French have such wonderful military art, but have never won a war?' Like magic, the publisher declared in English, 'You are not interested in these books', grabbed them up and departed hastily! That was a pity, for I had had an idea as to how to create something from them for our market.

1999 was my fortieth year at the Fair and I mentioned this in a letter to the Fair director, whom I knew from my London Book Fair days. A few weeks before the Fair I received a telephone call from the director's office inviting me to a reception. The problem was that I already had a very full diary, and to play for time whilst I checked my diary I commented 'how can I be invited to celebrate my fortieth year of the Frankfurt Book Fair when I am only thirty-seven?' There was a long pause, and one felt one could hear them thinking 'Are we dealing with an idiot, or is this English humour?' Eventually there came a cautious 'Haha, Mr Leventhal, yes, very good.' By this time I had checked my diary and we agreed the date for the reception. For that year my colleagues kindly made a presentation to me. John Taylor created a volume with a false cover around a blank volume entitled *Great Frankfurt Campaigns, 1959–1999*. The blurb on the front flap read in part:

'Here at last is an account by a combatant who has experienced at first hand the hurly burly, the huggermugger of campaigning in the Main valley over many seasons. Starting out as a humble foot-soldier, the author ... was soon in command of the Arms and Armour brigade. Over many years this unit descended on Frankfurt, striking fear into those who encountered them. Over the last fifteen years, however, the author has compounded the small, crack, elite Greenhill force ... and has wrought havoc of a different kind. He candidly reveals his strategy in this volume ... each day, he heads motorised sorties into Frankfurt itself, and having created mayhem during the day, withdraws, just as dusk is falling, to Kronberg. By night he leads his troops in much carousing in the local taverns, but returns refreshed and ready for the fray on the morrow. It is a remarkable account by any stretch of the imagination, fit to rank alongside Hannibal (of Alpine fame, not Lecter), T. E. Lawrence and Orde Wingate. If you want the real taste of Frankfurt (rather than simply frankfurters, sauerkraut and sekt), you will find it here.'

The blank volume was signed during the course of the Fair with greetings (on a non-compulsory basis, I assure you) by many friends who visited the stand.

One is often asked how to evaluate the importance of the Frankfurt Book Fair. In any 'book fair top ten' listing, Frankfurt would occupy the top five places. Having made so many visits over so many years one is asked upon one's return the inevitable questions whether it was a good fair, and how it compares to previous fairs, and which was the best Frankfurt Book Fair. Another question is 'Does it all become repetitive, and does one reinvent the wheel periodically?' I have to say that each year seems to be the best year ever. Each year is stimulating and there is something new and different (over the last few years it has been the reopening of the countries of Eastern Europe, and licensing books to the Czech Republic, Poland, Hungary and the old Soviet Union) and hence it is never repetitive or boring. If my first visit to the Frankfurt Book Fair was over forty years ago, I look forward to another possible forty years and do not see electronic means of communication in any way replacing the need to get together in person.

8

WORKING WITH THE SOVIETS, AND THE RUSSIANS

FOR MY GENERATION, a significant portion of our lives was dominated by the Cold War. Even as far back as my time with Herbert Jenkins I recall checking a mailing list of booksellers and finding on it the names of the Krogers, the husband and wife Soviet spies whose espionage activities were undertaken under the cover of being booksellers. The Cold War certainly influenced my publishing, ranging from *Russian Infantry Weapons of World War II* in 1971 to *Soviet Casualties and Combat Losses in the Twentieth Century* in 1998.

Although Russia and the Soviet Union have a rich and dramatic history, as a generalisation books on the subject sell less well than books on British, American or German military history. This was not so in the menacing days of the Cold War, when the Soviets were thought to be ten feet tall. In those days there was keen interest in anything about the Soviet Union, for there was a frisson of fear because of the possibility of conflict, but very little, if any, material came from there except in a pre-digested and denatured fashion. Since the fall of the Soviet Union so much material has become available that one could have sufficient for a whole new publishing house, but without that frisson it is of interest only to a limited circle.

I found working with the Soviets, in the days of the Cold War, easier in certain ways than working with the Russians in recent years. In the Cold War days you dealt with an official bureau, and indeed with bureaucrats, and what was set down was fixed and definite; in current times (excepting when working through our excellent, current Russian literary agent) there is lots of wheeling and dealing, and even when you think something is fixed and definite it may well not be.

In the late 1960s and early 1970s I had several small book import contracts, on the basis of which I imported into Britain, for international distribution, illustrated books with an English-language text about World War II from the Soviet Union. At about that time I had a liaison with a noted authority, Dr Leonid Tarassuk, who was the highly respected Keeper of Western Arms and Armour at the Hermitage in Leningrad. I published his *Russian Pistols in the 17th Century*, an academic study about firearms. Then his *Antique European and American Firearms at the Hermitage Museum* was published, a fine and handsome illustrated book on the museum's unique collection. I thought that this book would have good commercial potential for international distribution, but there was a problem. Dr Tarassuk was Jewish, and he waited until a few weeks after the book was published, and copies circulated to key fellow curators internationally, to file his papers to emigrate from the Soviet Union. Such an act would have been seen in those days as anti-Soviet, and would bring all sorts of repercussions upon the person who was seeking to emigrate, and Leonid immediately lost his job and the book was withdrawn from sale in the Soviet Union. Officially he was a non-person, and after all, how could somebody who no longer existed have his name on a book? This was the effect of applying to leave the Soviet Union.

It was at this point, in the bad days of the Cold War, that I got involved. Firstly, it was impractical for any of the international curators who knew him to run a lobby, from a museum, to try to apply pressure on the Soviet Union to permit him to emigrate, so I became the international anchorman for a campaign for his release (with Larry Wilson as my partner in the United States). There were enormous social problems in those days of the Cold War, and we set up a weekly telephone call to Leningrad so as to ensure that Leonid was still alive and had not been sent off to a camp in Siberia, arranged the smuggling via

Finland of drugs that his sick and elderly mother needed, and so forth. The regular telephone call, which would have been known about by the Soviet authorities, meant that Leonid could not disappear without our knowledge, as did others with similar problems. I remember one day when I was at home in bed with a nasty cold receiving a telephone call from Leonid in Leningrad who had a sudden, new and severe problem. This was before the days of direct dial telephone calls, but through the operator I telephoned Larry Wilson in Connecticut, who called a friend in Arizona who could reach Dr Henry Kissinger in Washington DC, received a call back in London, and closed the circle with Leningrad, all within four hours.

But back to books and business, and a second form of involvement, based on commercial judgement, was to seek to purchase the stock of Dr Tarassuk's book. An appointment was made and three Soviet visitors came to my Hampstead High Street offices. One was a representative of the Leningrad publishing house, the other was a representative of the Soviet Trade Delegation whom I knew from some other discussions, and the third was introduced as their associate, but he spoke no English.

Because I knew that many hours of discussion would be needed to make a purchase arrangement, again based on previous experience where, and very correctly, every sentence of a purchase contract would be discussed, I did not want to have such a long discussion only to receive a message a few days later to the effect that the matter would not be proceeded with.

I therefore put a copy of the book on to the desk and said 'I understand that the author has a problem. I hope that there is nothing that will prevent us from having a commercial transaction.' And waited for a response. And waited. There was a long, long silence. My point was that, obviously, if the author was now a non-person and did not exist, would that mean that his book would not be available, and therefore our discussion would waste a lot of time?

After a long pause I repeated the question.

A technique in interviewing, when there are questions and answers, is that if the interviewer pauses, and does not run on with another question, the person being interviewed will often fill the gap, and may even say something they did not mean to. Nobody spoke. We sat there silently.

Again time passed by. Then the gentleman who knew no English said 'Mr Leventhal, we are here to discuss a business matter and we are ready when you are.'

Obviously he was the political person sent to watch over the others, and they could say nothing whatsoever which could be interpreted in a political fashion. So it may well be that Leonid Tarassuk did not exist as far as they were concerned, but he was now a separate matter from a commercial situation.

As previously, the discussion took quite some time. At one point when we were discussing quantities and prices, they tried to get me to increase the quantity that we were willing to purchase. I said that we could do so, but only if the price was reduced. They saw no correlation between a lower retail price and an increase in sales.

A deal was struck, contract terms were negotiated, but it was going to take a short while for them to prepare the paperwork, have it authorised from Moscow, etc. They telephoned one Thursday in order to come over and have the paperwork signed. Unfortunately I was totally tied up with meetings and would be away from the office on the Friday. I said that I was willing to meet them at the weekend, because there was pressure on them to get the paperwork to Moscow so as to fulfil the requirements for their quarterly budget. 'Do you work at the weekend?' I was asked with surprise. 'Yes, if I have to: I am a capitalist,' I responded. 'What time would you like us to be with you, Mr Leventhal?' And they came into the office at 9.30 on a Sunday morning, and the paperwork was signed and flown that day to Moscow.

After all of that, I am glad to say that the book was successful and sold out. Also successful was the campaign to obtain emigration visas for Leonid and his family, but that's another, long story.

In one of my meetings in those days of the Cold War with the Soviet Trade Delegation, during general conversation, which was somewhat difficult with them, I showed the delegation our new book *Russian Tanks 1900–1970* by John Milsom. This was a substantial and illustrated volume, and I said that we were interested in works of a similar nature and asked if they had any such books that we should consider for translation. Great surprise was expressed that such books were of interest, and that there was an audience for them. One of the team mentioned that he had fought in tanks during the Great Patriotic War, but had never ever seen a book on the subject. He seemed to turn over the pages with such interest, and wistful reminiscence, that I presented him with the book. It took us something like twenty years to see similar material from Russia, and by then the market had changed.

Other transactions over the years have included the large-format illustrated book *The Great Patriotic War*, for which we obtained a very large number of photographs, edited by Peter Tsouras. The full story about *Soviet Wings* is told in Chapter 17. This project started in the last days of the old Soviet Union and concluded at the time of its collapse. The book was, I believe, not published in the Soviet Union, and for the Moscow publishing house with which we were dealing it represented something of a new and unusual transaction. Although the photographer was very much involved with the preparation of the project, and providing unique and wonderful images to our specification, after the book had been published and after we had started paying monies we received a writ in Russian from a

Moscow court. It appeared that the Moscow publishing house with which we were working had not obtained a contract that permitted licensing this material in a foreign language. We chose not to get involved in the litigation that appeared to be going on between the publisher and photographer, and solved the matter by holding up any payments until the parties there had got their act together, and we received instructions from both of them, jointly, for the payment of monies.

There was an official Moscow bureau for licensing the international rights to books by Soviet authors. This was also, going back to Cold War days, a way of controlling what was made available for international sale, because in Soviet law it was a criminal offence not to use the official bureau. This is why dissidents or those whose writings did not conform with Soviet policy could not get their books offered internationally, or if they did could be sent to jail or into exile. The official bureau continued, however, with the transition from the Cold War to the new age, but changed its name, and had to work within a commercial framework. We have had a number of discussions over the years with the bureau and with a contract through them translated the large-format, superbly illustrated *Illustrated Encyclopedia of Handguns* by A. B. Zhuk. Again, the author was enormously helpful and we enjoyed a good direct correspondence with him, and received a warm letter of thanks from him on the publication of the book.

We were getting ready to start the very difficult job of undertaking a second volume when we received a letter from the author cancelling the contract. This caused consternation. We had an official contract. The author knew all about it. Everyone knew all about it. It appeared, however, that an American visiting Moscow had reached the author, and persuaded him that he could do a better job than we could. There were discussions with the official authors' bureau but staff shrugged their shoulders. We were in touch with those in Britain who are familiar with Soviet copyright law, but there were all the problems as to how to pursue the matter. I pointed out to the authors' bureau that such cancellation meant that none of its contracts had any value whatsoever. Again they shrugged. It is possible that this was due to the author's being a high-ranking military official, which was of course how he had accessed the weapons for illustration purposes. So we either had to pursue the matter through the neutral court in Sweden, or step aside. With enormous regret we chose the latter course, and stepped aside, but now some five years later there is still no sight of the American edition that caused the cancellation of ours.

Yesteryear, in the days of the Cold War, almost anything on a Soviet military subject would attract a lot of attention and sell well. With peace, and without the possibility of conflict, this is no longer the case. Hence when recently we undertook a very fine reference work, full of most valuable information and an extremely difficult translation job, *Soviet Casualties and Combat Losses in the Twentieth Century*, its sales were sadly lamentable.

I nearly made a visit behind the Iron Curtain in 1973 when Leonid Tarassuk and his family were to be flown to freedom (or exile, I guess, from the Soviet viewpoint) from Moscow via Budapest to Vienna. As refugees arriving in Vienna were not permitted to circulate or have access to the public, because this was a sensitive matter, I planned to fly into Budapest on the flight arriving shortly before the Aeroflot flight from Moscow, and change on to it so that I could meet Leonid and his family. A friend with intelligence connections thought that advice was desirable, and word came back that my name would be known to those who monitor arrivals because of my involvement in the campaign to release Leonid and I would not be welcome, and would have a rather unpleasant time. Hence I cancelled my plan, and have waited until recently to visit modern Russia and when time had passed such matters by. My wife and I enjoyed a vacation on a ship that cruised in the Baltic, and we were able to spend three days in St Petersburg. We visited Dr Tarassuk's Hermitage Museum, which is a most wonderful establishment full of treasure housed in astonishing buildings. Now Russia welcomes visitors, but it was sad to see this great city, with its rich and dramatic history, in a run-down condition.

9

GOING TO AMERICA

THANKS ARE DUE TO THE SOCIETY OF YOUNG PUBLISHERS for my first visit to the United States. In 1961 they secured funding for two of their members to go to New York. Applicants were to send in a paper setting down why they wanted to go (a silly question: New York was seen as the most exciting and glamorous place on the planet) and to be interviewed. Yes, I really, really wanted to go. No, I was not chosen.

Herbert Jenkins had supported my application. I think that there had been only two post-war visits by Derek Grimsdick to New York, but he and his colleagues decided that there should be another visit by a representative of the company. Spurred by the desire I had shown to go under the aegis of the Society of Young Publishers, they decided that I should go.

So it was that in October 1961 I flew off (in a plane with propellers) to New York for three weeks. I stayed at a very large, low-cost hotel far over on West 58th. I only stayed there the once, because the hotel was far from the centre and the area went into decline, and the hotel closed.

I knew no-one at that point over there, and it was very lonely at times. I was very busy during the daytime, but it was awfully quiet in the evenings and at the weekends, with nobody to talk to. Hence one of the things I did was to play tourist. I took the Circle Line cruise around Manhattan, went up the Empire State Building, visited the United Nations Building and so forth. New York bus and subway fares at that time were fifteen cents, and I believe that subway tokens would have been a great investment, if only one could have stock-piled them, for nowadays they cost $1.50. During that first trip I learned that the 'No Standing' sign at bus stops related to cars and not those waiting for the buses, that the 'Fine for Parking' sign was not a kind invitation, and that when doing arithmetic with a pencil in a meeting and trying to make a correction one does not ask for a rubber. I was also able to go to the theatre, because in those days I had no evening engagements (does anyone else remember *The Unsinkable Molly Brown* and *Fiorello?*) and cinema (seeing *Breakfast at Tiffany's*, which has a scene set in the New York Public Library at Fifth and 42nd, one of the places I had visited that day), but have never had the time for theatre or cinema since then. I ate at the local Horn and Hardart, a Woolworths-style cafeteria with a bank of glass boxes from which one's meal could be selected (I eat rather differently nowadays).

Every day I wrote a letter reporting on my activities, addressing it 'Dear Mr Grimsdick and Dear Mr Eagle' (this being after I had already worked with them for five years). Reviewing these, I see that I wrote forty pages with daily detail, packing into the three weeks meetings with 105 people at ninety publishing houses. How the publishing scene has changed over the years: amongst the firms I visited were independent, stand-alone houses which were well-known and innovative back then, but are now long-since out of business and forgotten, or a mere imprint as part of a conglomerate, such as:

Fleet Publishing	Channel Press	Grosset & Dunlap
Thomas Yoseloff/	Devin-Adair	Hastings House
A. S. Barnes	Frederick Fell	Julian Messner
Ivan Obolensky	Tudor	Philosophical Press
Hearthside Press	Ronald Press	University Press
Fawcett	Duell, Sloan &	Bernard Geis
Hill and Wang	Pearce	Rudo Globus
Orion Press	Julian Press	

As an aside, these above were all firms that I visited and either did business with or tried to, and there are others that could be added to the listing of 'disappeared US publishing houses'. This is not however a unique situation for the United States; I am sure that a list just as long could be drawn up of British publishers who were once innovative, and had a regular publishing programme, and have gone out of business over the years.

Hearthside Press offered us the first cookery book that was based on a novel slimming regime, but we turned this down. Who in Britain had ever heard of Weight Watchers, and such a slimming plan could never work for our sort of audience, could it? It was whilst I was talking to the husband-and-wife team who ran Hearthside Press that they mentioned the forthcoming Hallowe'en evening. At that time Hallowe'en was unknown in Great Britain, and there was certainly no concept of children going around to play 'Trick or Treat'. It is only over subsequent years, following many American films and television programmes, that Hallowe'en has become part of British culture. I was invited to their home at Long Island, for dinner and to go 'Trick or Treating' with their children. People thought I had a wonderful disguise as an English gentleman!

The timing of my visit was, with the benefit of hindsight, most fortunate in being at the beginning of the great days of co-edition sales from British publishers to the United States, which also triggered a number of return deals. The heyday of the co-edition lasted through the 1960s and 1970s, but faltered shortly afterwards, due to changing business patterns, although a number of publishers still do some co-edition business.

One of the people I met with at that time was Milton Gladstone of Arco. In my daily letter back home I reported:

'3.00. ARCO. Saw Milton Gladstone. Had a very interesting conversation with this man which I think should be most fruitful. He expressed interest in a number of our books and I am returning to his office on Monday to continue our talk and to see his books.'

This contact led to many years of friendship, and mutual good business. Arco bought co-editions of all the Herbert

Jenkins books on firearms, and were subsequently remarkably supportive when I came to undertake publishing at Arms & Armour Press. Arco for many years was probably one of the largest American importers of British co-editions, on a wide range of non-fiction subjects. The results of all of the many, many meetings I had, and relationships I established, created a worthwhile number of transactions, with books being added to the Herbert Jenkins list and books sold to US publishers. Hence I went over again in 1963 and see that my letters at that time continued to be addressed: 'Dear Mr Grimsdick', and some separately to 'Dear Mr Eagle'. I had by then been working with them for seven years. This trip was for a longer period of time – a month – and also included a couple of days in Toronto, via the Niagara Falls on a freezing, viciously cold day.

Again I was extremely active in getting around as much as I could, because the Herbert Jenkins list was of a very wide and general nature and there were many, many publishers to discuss books with. Where books on military history and firearms were concerned, I see from my correspondence the pursuit of quite a number of such and a meeting on 17 April 1963:

'FOLLETT. Discussed our distribution of *Gun Digest* and the other books on firearms that they distribute. Will be speaking to them again.'

Herbert Jenkins did subsequently undertake such distribution, and my relationship with *Gun Digest* has continued over many years. Digest Books Inc, the publishers, became DBI Books Inc, was sold to Dunn & Bradstreet, who later sold the firm to the firm's vigorous executives Chuck Hartigan and John Strauss, who eventually sold it to Krause of Iola, Wisconsin.

Another relationship that continues to the present was with Stackpole Books and on Monday 29 April I report:

'STACKPOLE. Had a long talk with their Sales Director. I think that we will now be able to take their titles on a really exclusive basis. Possibilities that they may be interested in taking some of our future books but these are slight.'

In the early 1960s it was really special to go to New York. New York had yet to be invaded by the British, and for many people their only familiarity with the English accent was from films or David Frost, and I probably could have used his name to sign bills in restaurants for I was frequently asked if I was him. The accent also had a great effect on young ladies. From the British viewpoint, it was so unusual to be able to go to New York that one's views of America and opinion of American society were eagerly sought. The British perception of the United States in general, and of New York in particular, is likewise from films and television, and this gives it a glamour which, for a period, I was very happy to have rub off a little on me. My first visit coincided with Kennedy being President. These were the days of Camelot (both on the stage, but also with Kennedy's glamorous wife in Washington DC).

One characteristic of New York is the afternoon change of shift by taxi-cab drivers. Woe betide you if you are trying to catch a taxi at that time. One time I was trying to catch a taxi at 4pm from downtown at 20th Street to get uptown to 50th Street, much too far to walk, and was somewhat anxious and already late for a meeting. All of the taxis zoomed past with their 'Off Duty' signs alight, and I started to indicate that I wanted to go in their direction heading off duty by standing in the middle of the road and thumbing a lift and pointing at myself. A taxi stopped and said that he would take me part of the way because it was in his direction for going off duty. I jumped in and endeavoured to get a longer ride from the driver by starting a conversation. Encouraging the driver to talk, reckoning that the longer that he talked the closer to the destination he would take me, it was soon revealed that the taxi driver had served in the British Army for twelve years. Where? Mainly with the 151st Highland Division, especially in North Africa and Italy.

There was a discussion about Rommel (which I based on publishing books such as *Rommel: Battles and Campaigns* by Kenneth Macksey and Rommel's own *Infantry Attacks*) and it turned out that the driver had, he claimed, participated in the abortive raid to kill Rommel. How about tanks? The driver had seen service in Valentines and Matildas, and so a copy of *British Tank Markings and Names* was pulled from my briefcase and shown to him. At each intersection and traffic jam, gradually progressing in the required direction, the driver looked through the book and expressed delight at seeing the tanks that he remembered so well. 'Where can I obtain a copy of this book?' he asked. The answer, as we finally arrived at the required address, was immediately 'with the compliments of the publisher'.

Forty years on, New York is still stimulating and exciting, and one can feel the electricity in the streets. Physically, in fact, New York has changed little over the years, and although there have been new skyscrapers built, one tall building looks very much like another. Thus the only real changes to the basic profile of the City have been when the new PanAm building blocked the vista of Park Avenue, and then of course the terrible destruction of the World Trade Center. Even the hotel I stayed in on my first visit has been resurrected and become the fashionable Ian Schrager, Philippe Starck-designed Hudson.

It was those early visits to New York that made me realise what London meant to me, and London's human scale. It is in fact London which has become more exciting over the years, evolving into a 24-hour city which is hot with activity and cool with style, and dynamic with a never-ending stream of new buildings, restaurants and cultural activity.

10

AN AMERICAN
RELATIONSHIP

MY LONG-STANDING RELATIONSHIP WITH STACKPOLE BOOKS has been in three portions.

The first was when I was working for Herbert Jenkins, which had a modest list of books on sporting subjects, including shooting. In the Spring of 1958 we started importing and distributing the books on firearms published by Stackpole. These included classic works such as *Hatcher's Notebook* by Major General Julian S. Hatcher, *Firearms Investigation, Identification and Evidence* by Hatcher, Jury and Weller, and *Gas, Air and Spring Guns of the World* by W. H. B. Smith, which continued to sell for many years. Herbert Jenkins progressed with building quite a list of books on shooting as a sport, including those from Stackpole Books and then publications by DBI Books (such as *Gun Digest*), and, in 1960, started publishing new books on antique firearms. Then in 1965 Herbert Jenkins was taken over, and I departed.

The second began shortly after I founded Arms & Armour Press. I was in touch again with Stackpole Books, and this led to a co-edition relationship, with them taking many valuable new books for US publication, beginning with:

1968 *Rapiers* by Eric Valentine
1969 *Flintlock Pistols* by F. J. Wilkinson
    Japanese Armour by John Anderson
    German Tanks of World War II by F. M. von Senger und Etterlin
1970 *Scottish Swords and Dirks* by John Wallace
    Naval Swords by P. G. W. Annis
1971 *German Pistols and Revolvers* by Ian V. Hogg

1972 *Pictorial History of Tanks of the World* by Peter Chamberlain and Chris Ellis

It was our work together on these books that helped to establish Arms & Armour Press and our collaboration continued in this way for about a decade, until I decided not to supply books to the United States as co-editions, but to keep the whole Arms & Armour Press list together and work on a distribution basis. This decision came gradually over a period of time because of the problems of having to break up one's publishing list across a number of US publishing houses in order to get books on sale over there, and there was always a residue which was not sold at all in the United States. I decided it would be better to have the whole list kept together, to preserve identity and also to ensure that all of our authors had their books on sale in this important market. As this decision evolved, one year, in the latter half of the 1970s, my wife and I were on vacation in Southern California enjoying touring, and we visited a quiet little place called La Jolla. We day-dreamed about how nice it would be if we were able to create a relationship on a distribution basis with a publisher who was in a place of a similar nature, and we might even be able to take an apartment and spend time there in order to work more closely with them. Apartments didn't seem that expensive.

A little time passed, and a distribution relationship between Arms & Armour Press and Stackpole Books was formed. A few years later my wife was again with me when we were visiting publishers, and having a brief break, in the United States. We were in New York and she looked at my schedule and saw that we had a busy, long day ahead of us. We were to go out to Newark at about 7am, catch a commuter flight to Harrisburg in central Pennsylvania, work there until the early afternoon, and then rent a car and drive south for about four hours to West Virginia where we were to have our break. 'This seems to be a long day, Lionel,' Elizabeth said to me. 'Isn't Harrisburg the La Jolla of the East Coast?' I told her to wait and see and after our visit she understood why, notwithstanding the nice people who were there, I had chosen that we should go somewhere else for a vacation.

Arms & Armour Press also distributed a number of books from Stackpole, including their monumental *Small Arms of the World*, and we reprinted in a British edition *Gas, Air and Spring Guns*. It was when we were advised that *Small Arms of the World*, of which we had sold a remarkable number, was not going to be published in a revised edition that we undertook its British counterpart *Military Small Arms of the 20th Century* by Ian V. Hogg and John Weeks, first published in 1973 and which has been continually in print, in successive new editions, since then (a seventh edition has been published by Krause).

The relationship with Stackpole was a close one, and I would visit Harrisburg every time I was in the United States. Depending upon my tour I was sometimes faced with a 'you can't get there from here' situation, combined with problems of timescale. A pattern evolved and I would find myself having to travel between Annapolis and Harrisburg, which can't be done by train or by scheduled flight. However Tom Epley, the Press Director of the Naval Institute, would use his Cessna 172 to fly me up from a nearby airport to Harrisburg, or vice versa, this giving me a direct and very speedy route. A friend from Stackpole Books would then collect me from the private hangar area at Harrisburg.

It was, however, on a commuter jet from Newark that I learned the hard lesson that one should not fly with a cold, as I did on that occasion, without taking a decongestant. I suffered excruciating pain in my ears, and came off the plane totally deaf. Awaiting me were the two executives from Stackpole Books, and I had to gesture to them my problem. They took me to a neighbouring coffee shop where they got me something to drink and started looking at papers, but it was an hour or two before we could actually converse. Since then, whenever I have been speaking to somebody who seems to have a cold and who I know is going to be taking a flight, I always warn them about the problems that can be experienced with one's ears and advise that they should take a decongestant.

That stage of the relationship with Stackpole lasted until my sale of Arms & Armour Press in October 1984, when Link House Books switched the agency to another US publisher. A side beneficiary of this was Osprey, for Stackpole had gained experience selling pictorial paperbacks with the several Arms & Armour Press series such as *Warbirds Illustrated, Tanks Illustrated, Uniforms Illustrated* etc., and as Osprey were seeking US distribution for their books of a similar format (10 inches x 7.5 inches) they filled the gap left by Arms & Armour Press's moving on, until quite recently.

The A&AP list was switched to Sterling Books of New York, who distributed Blandford and the other Link House Books imprints. One advantage of the switch was their extremely professional seasonal sales conferences held at the Windows on the World at the top of the World Trade Center.

Although I didn't work directly with Stackpole after the switch, the contact certainly continued. One very friendly means of maintaining contact has been, and is, with Judith Schnell, their Editorial Director, who always stays in the same hotel as the Greenhill team in Kronberg, during the Frankfurt Book Fair. At one point it was necessary to change hotels, and although we had identified that the Hotel Schutzenhof had been refurbished and reopened we did not stay in it in its first year, but recommended it instead to Judith for her first visit to Kronberg and Frankfurt. We, unfortunately, chose a different hotel that year, which was deservedly in its last year, as we discovered to our enormous discomfort, and we switched the following year to the Schutzenhof. By then Judith had established occupancy of the best room in the hotel that had been our find, and this continues to this day.

As Greenhill Books grew we bought a number of books on a co-edition basis from Stackpole, notably the fine series on American Army uniforms by Shelby Stanton.

Again, as the new Greenhill Books list grew, it was distributed in the United States through our friends at Presidio, but at the Frankfurt Book Fair in 1992 Judith discussed with us certain books of theirs that we might undertake on a co-edition basis. She looked at the Greenhill books and said that if we ever chose to depart from Presidio we should bear Stackpole in mind. This was almost a case of precognition because shortly after that Presidio advised that they were changing their sales and distribution, and hence we could no longer be under their wing. I was immediately in touch with Marianne Baier, the Vice-President in charge of sales, at Stackpole Books, and visited the offices for the first time in a number of years (driving up from DC in a dangerous snow storm). As from mid-Spring of 1993 Greenhill undertook the international sale of Stackpole Books on military history, and in June 1993 they reciprocated by becoming Greenhill's US distributors, and this relationship – the third stage – continues to the present.

Over the years I have worked with a number of different people at Stackpole Books, rather depending upon whether I was dealing with the sales or the editorial side. In the key period of initial Arms & Armour Press work, Jim Reitmulder was in overall charge until he died suddenly in 1972. As Stackpole expanded Glenn Johns came in during the late 1970s, and created new roles for three who have since had long careers at Stackpole: Judith Schnell, Marianne Baier and Donna Pope. After Glenn, and his Chief Executive Hank Hamill, David Detweiler got more involved with the management, and Judith Schnell took over the editorial side with Marianne Baier on sales and marketing. Marianne retired in 1997. Stackpole have always had specific managers to sell to the specialist markets, and the manager in charge of military book accounts is Peter Rossi, who has long experience of the book trade.

I visit Stackpole every year, meet with the sales team at Book-Expo America (aka ABA) and continue to get together with Judith Schnell in Frankfurt (and her colleague Leigh Ann Berry, who also visits London in the Spring for the London Book Fair).

The team at Stackpole with whom we at Greenhill liaise includes:

David Detweiler: Chairman
David Ritter: President and Chief Operating Executive
Judith Schnell: Vice-President and Editorial Director
Leigh Ann Berry: History Editor
Pat Moran: Director of Sales and Marketing
Peter Rossi: Sales Manager (History, Library)
Donna Pope: Specialty Accounts Manager
Colonel Edward Skender, USA (Ret.): Military Reference
Susan Drexler: Manager, Order Entry, Customer Service
and Shipping

and others with whom we work include Vicki Brewer (marketing) and Adrian Fleming (warehouse).

11

ARMS & ARMOUR PRESS:
THE GLORY YEARS

WHEN I SIGNED THE LEASE on the yet-to-be built offices at 2–6 Hampstead High Street, I didn't realise how advantageous it was, and it took a further eighteen months before the building was ready for occupancy. During that time office rentals had taken a great leap forward again, and the rent we were able to charge for the half space that we sublet brought us a profit on the whole; for a number of years we effectively had rent-free accommodation. One year an audit clerk queried that the accounts he was working on were obviously incomplete because they did not include rent; was something wrong? I agreed: yes, we should have been making a profit.

Hampstead is one of London's most pleasant (and today) costly areas to work and live in. Underneath our offices was Ian Norrie's famous High Hill Bookshop, and within 100 yards were many restaurants at which authors or other guests could be entertained. A favourite was the Villa Bianca where, even through I dined sometimes twice a week, they would not stock tea to make me lemon tea to finish a meal. I would take a tea bag with me, and at the end of a meal the waiter could come discreetly to me with a plate on to which I put it, and he would go off and make my lemon tea.

By the time Arms & Armour Press moved into its Hampstead High Street offices in 1971 the publishing programme had some eighteen new titles being released each year, a number that remained fairly stable for the next four or five years, although the content of the books increased. Even to select highlights is difficult but included on any short-list would have to be:

Who Dares Wins by Tony Geraghty

Military Small Arms of the 20th Century by Ian V. Hogg
and John Weeks
Atlas of Military Strategy by David G. Chandler
British Battleships of World War Two by Alan Raven and
John Roberts
British Cruisers of World War Two by Alan Raven and
John Roberts
The Rapier and Small Sword, 1400-1820 by A. V. B.
Norman
Encyclopedia of German Tanks of World War Two by Peter
Chamberlain, Hilary L. Doyle and Thomas Jentz
Tanks of the World, 1914-1945 by Peter Chamberlain and
Chris Ellis
German Army Uniforms & Insignia by Brian L. Davis
The Armour of Imperial Rome by H. Russell Robinson
Combat Aircraft of World War Two by Elke C. Weal, John
A. Weal and Richard F. Baker
Luger by John Walter
Modern Soviet Armour by Steven Zaloga

A number of these books and others from that period continue
to be in print.

In the early 1970s we had a student undertake some work
experience for us. He was both very knowledgeable and an
excellent researcher, and the result of his summertime work
was published as *British Military Uniforms 1768-1796*, sub-
titled *The Dress of the British Army from Contemporary Sources*.
The student was Hew Strachan, now Chichele Professor of the
History of War at Oxford (and Fellow of All Souls).

The publishing programme grew, the number of titles
published each year being:

1966: two   1968: ten   1970: seventeen
1967: eight   1969: nineteen   1971: eighteen

1972: nineteen	1976: twenty	1980: thirty-two
1973: fourteen	1977: twenty-four	1981: twenty-eight
1974: twenty-one	1978: twenty-three	
1975: sixteen	1979: twenty-seven	

The simple figures really need further qualification in order to present a true picture, for it makes an awful lot of difference to bare figures if monograph reprints of out-of-print material are compared, for the purpose of a statistical number of titles, with a wholly new major illustrated reference work. Hence, although it may have taken five or ten years to double title output, the size and content of the books quadrupled, octupled and multiplied tenfold.

The early 1970s also saw the launch of the Military Book Club, which has grown to become an essential part of the military publishing scene, and Arms & Armour Press participated from the very beginning. We were astonished and concerned when one of our books was used as a 'lead' ('send 2/6d and get the book ...') but there was no correlation between their offer and sales in the bookshops.

Commencing in 1975 Arms & Armour Press organised a number of events and lectures to help foster interest in military subjects (and also to sell books). Memorable are:

¶ Waterloo Day: a phenomenal success, held on the hottest day of the year in June 1975, to promote the publication of *Waterloo* by Henri Lachouque. This was the progenitor of the current International Napoleonic Fair.

¶ America's Military Heritage, 1776–1976: a terrible failure.

¶ Firearms Symposia: two took place at the Tower of London.

¶ Napoleonic Symposia: a series with lectures (Dr David

Chandler regularly participated) and films, used to launch books such as the first reprinting of *The Anatomy of Glory.*

Especially memorable were the RAF Museum Symposia. We held seven or eight of these events at the Royal Air Force Museum in Hendon and speakers included Sir Arthur 'Bomber' Harris, and Battle of Britain air aces Stanford Tuck, Douglas Bader, Johnnie Johnson, and 'Don' Bennett. These were to promote the RAF Museum Series and I had the privilege of lunching the speakers, and that was when I met Sir Arthur Harris, which led to my reprinting his *Bomber Offensive* and eventually to the publication of *Bomber Harris: His Life and Times* by Henry Probert. Sir Arthur was a short, modest-looking person, but when he spoke to the audience (in fact about World War I aviation, not Bomber Command in World War II) there was an electric atmosphere and he was the only speaker to receive a standing ovation. The other time an audience rose to its feet was when there was the first ever showing of a unique, hitherto unknown colour film of a Lancaster squadron being trained, and then raiding Berlin. This film had been shot over a period of months by the commander of a base, Air Commodore H. I. Cozens, and it had never been shown publicly before. The RAF Museum had researched and brought together again the whole of the crew, who had never seen the film, and they were invited to the showing and showed up in their Sunday best, together with their families. The crew were, to their total surprise, invited on to the platform after the film, and one had the 'before and after' effect of seeing them as young men going off for the arduous Lancaster bombing raids, and as middle-aged men on the stage. They epitomised youth going off to war, without honour or glory, and the audience stood for them.

Admission was charged for all these events, and many books were sold. Sometimes using facilities with limited seating the cost of admission was raised a little, for we found that if people paid they were more likely to attend and not be a 'no show'. For some events there was a waiting list, or standing room only, and some visitors would especially come over from the Continent. Lectures and autographing events were also held at the prestigious Royal United Services Institute in Whitehall, with Charles Beckwith talking about his book *Delta Force* and the attempt to rescue the American hostages in Teheran (and which led to a full, front-page story in one of the tabloids, but it didn't sell any books), Chaim Herzog talking about the Arab–Israeli Wars, and others.

In addition to such exclusively Arms & Armour Press events, for several years Arms & Armour Press instigated and organised the Spring Military Book Campaign, a successful national British publishers' co-operative promotion. Autographing sessions and author tours were arranged, and there were interviews of authors on radio and television. We had our own arrangement for creating an author interview and circulating a tape to radio stations. One author who went on a tour was Kenneth Macksey to promote *Invasion: The German Invasion of England, July 1940*. At an autographing event in Maidstone a young, local person was buying a copy of the book for his father and was sure that his father had participated in the German attack on Maidstone although he had never spoken about it.

I made the mistake of once mentioning to an author that, although I was a military publisher, I had never fired a gun. I was visiting with the American firearms expert Larry Wilson in his home in Connecticut. He had a very handsome, unusual study which was double level, double height, with a Ferrari racing car (of course), and an alcove with a full-sized stagecoach. Around the walls there was a collection of guns, and I knew sufficient about them from books to appreciate their significance when he mentioned particular items. When I said that I had never fired a gun, Larry pulled down a very large, double-barrelled shotgun used for shooting African game and took me out on to his patio. There was plenty of space, as far as the eye could see, and he said he would show me how to fire such a gun. I demurred. I certainly didn't want to end up with a broken or very bruised shoulder, whilst on a tour around America. But he showed me the stance and he test-fired it, and then he positioned me very carefully and I too fired the gun. Obviously it had been used in that area before, because it was very effective and there was no sign of any African game. The footnote to this story was that I kept the metal cartridge shell, and happened to have it in my coat as I passed through security at the airport on my way out. To them there was no difference between a full and empty shell, and although I tried to explain it was easier to leave my souvenir with them.

A diversion to the Arms & Armour Press publishing was the use of the considerable skills of the in-house editorial and production team to produce some exceptional full colour co-editions sold for simultaneous release in a number of countries. With the advent of colour printing for mass market co-editions I believed that there would be a market for using such techniques for books with a scientific or technical basis for international audiences, and created two fine and valuable works of scientific merit and one of a popular nature:

Butterflies of the World, with 6,200 butterflies illustrated in full colour. The first print run was approximately 60,000 copies, and the book has been reprinted two or three times since then (called in the office 'Butterflies of World War II').

Encyclopedia of World Stamps, with nearly 5,000 stamps in full colour.

Marine Life, with 1,300 colour photographs being reproduced.

The progression of sales of a publishing house is (or should be) cumulative. Those for Arms & Armour Press showed a consistent compound growth, rarely less than twenty per cent per annum; it was the best of times. There were also a number of painful lessons, as when we had to break off an inefficient third-party computerised invoicing system, which was then moved to another servicer who could not cope, and we finally had to bring the whole operation in house. The growth that we experienced created pressure, but had it not been for the growth then the constipation of computerised invoicing could have put us out of business. We eventually found an efficient third-party facility, and I have never ever tried again to have invoicing and sales accounting in house.

The last year of the seventies saw Mrs Thatcher become Prime Minister and start the fight against restrictive unions, and in 1981 the fairy tale wedding of Prince Charles to Lady Diana Spencer took place. The early 1980s also saw something of a recession in Great Britain, but Arms & Armour Press was immune to it because of the remarkable success of *Who Dares Wins* and several other books about special forces, together with the growth of the market in which we were publishing. Arms & Armour Press continued to grow, and at one time had twenty-five people employed in Hampstead, our own staff plus those in the Ken Trotman military bookshop.

We had twice-yearly sales meetings with the whole sales team, and invited in authors (encouraged to bring exhibits relating to the new book that they were presenting) and some key customers. One summer I double-booked a family holiday with the sales meeting. We were to vacation in the far west of Wales, near St David's. The timing of trains was not practical and would have needed two overnight journeys. There was a little airport at nearby Haverfordwest but in fact no flights to London. Doing some lateral thinking, I telephoned the flying club at Swansea and asked if one could rent a plane. No, planes were not available for rent. But I could pay for a lesson for somebody, who would be very happy to have free flying time and the extra hours on his log book. He would fly up, with an instructor, from Swansea to Haverfordwest, pick me up, and fly me across Britain to Leavesdon airport, just near Watford and only a few miles from the office. This happened, and I flew out in the morning, attended the sales meeting and lunch, and came back in the early evening in time for dinner. When some friends queried where I had been that day and I said 'London' there was a severe credibility gap, because it was just not possible to get there and back in a day.

For a period of years we closed the office one day each summer for an outing. These started quite modestly but grew into pleasant expeditions, such as along the Thames by small boat to Kew for lunch, with a guided tour around the Royal Botanical Gardens.

It was in 1984 I decided to take a capital gain. We had over the years been approached by several other publishers who were interested in acquiring Arms & Armour Press, and I entered into a discussion with Link House Books, who had a number of publishing imprints (most notably Blandford) under their umbrella. A deal was agreed on the eve of the Frankfurt Book Fair in 1984.

Link House Books were themselves the subject of a take-over as the Link House Magazine Group, of which it was part, was purchased by United Newspapers just a few weeks later. At the time that Arms & Armour Press joined the Link House Group books represented about ten per cent of their sales, but with the Link House Group joining United Newspapers the book division represented about one per cent of sales, and excepting only for Arms & Armour Press, was causing some commercial problems. I had hoped that there would be a continuing role but there was a move to consolidate all the book publishing, and hence functions were moved from Hampstead to Poole in Dorset, and eventually there was total integration with no need for the Hampstead High Street offices. Or Lionel Leventhal. This process took about two years. I was sorry that thereafter there was no contact at all with me, but I have over the years carried on watching the list, and still see books that I created and published stay in print, or be reprinted, and authors I brought to the list continue to be published and flourish.

Arms & Armour Press was in the right position at the right time: the right position was military book publishing, mainly 'nuts and bolts', and it was the right time because there was an enormous growth of interest in the subject area both in Britain, the Commonwealth and, especially and most fortunately, on a co-edition basis in the United States. By producing top quality books which have also stood the test of time Arms & Armour Press rode the crest of a most successful wave.

The first Arms & Armour Press books were published in October 1966 and I left twenty years later in October 1986. When I left I was proud of the publishing list, and the imprint was the leading one in military book publishing.

12

QUALITY BOOKSELLING

THE LEADING, LONGEST ESTABLISHED specialist military bookseller for books on arms and armour is Ken Trotman. I first got to know Ken in the late 1950s when I worked with him at Herbert Jenkins. He was so very helpful when I started Arms & Armour Press, then things changed radically and I took over the Trotman business in 1976 and was involved with it for eight years. I have a continuing relationship with the business today under the ownership of Richard and Roz Brown.

The origins of the Ken Trotman business go back earlier, and when we were preparing an announcement about the business being run under the Arms & Armour Press umbrella in Hampstead, Ken's wife Marie reminisced:

'It all goes back to 1947 and 1948. A friend who knew Ken from his school days asked him if he would be interested in joining a book business. Ken thought about it, although at the time he did not know anything at all about books on hunting, shooting and fishing. He sold his sports car for £100 and invested the money in books, and everything started from there. Ken learned as he went along, travelling all over England visiting all sorts of bookshops. This was done in his spare time as his main job was with British European Airways at Northolt.

'After a little while his partner married and moved to Ringwood in Hampshire, and Ken and I married and moved to High Wycombe, so the problem arose as to how to continue the business. Ken and his business partner parted, Ken taking the arms and armour section and his partner taking the hunting and fishing section.

'Business grew and Ken decided to leave BEA in 1953 as he found his book business was in fact growing to such an extent that he could not do two jobs for much longer. And so he went from strength to strength over the years, and made many good friends around the world.'

My association with Ken started because we believed at Herbert Jenkins that readers of magazines such as the *Shooting Times* were not regular habitués of bookshops and we wanted to promote our new books on shooting by mail-order advertising. Hence we cast around for a bookseller who could handle books on shooting and firearms, and Ken Trotman was unique in this respect. We took a series of large advertisements, which continued for some time because the response was wonderful. This certainly kept Ken very busy indeed, and he became an increasingly important account to Herbert Jenkins, and as Jenkins started importing American books on firearms (such as those from Stackpole Books, in Spring 1958, and then DBI Books a few years later) the association and friendship grew. When I undertook the publication at Herbert Jenkins of their first books on historic aspects of firearms, these fitted in with the relationship but also better complemented Ken's own regular sales to collectors.

After I left Herbert Jenkins, following the firm's being taken over in 1964, I maintained contact with him especially because of my increasing unhappiness at being removed from books at Paul Hamlyn. It was during the course of the following year that I determined I would not be staying at Hamlyn, but had no idea of the direction I should take. In conversation with Ken he mentioned some of the nineteenth-century source items on the history of firearms that he thought he could sell well, at the Arms Fairs he attended, and also through his mailing list. Initially these were to be reprints from journals such as that published by the Royal United Services Institute, and I costed these with a short-run printer and invited Ken to suggest how many copies he could take at a given cost. He said that he could take 100 copies of each, and my arithmetic showed that this would pay the printer's bill for 300 copies. Also Ken would pay for his 100 copies within the time that I needed to pay the printer. This led to the start of Arms & Armour Press.

As Arms & Armour Press grew, so the relationship with Ken Trotman continued to grow. I was always very happy to be in touch with him to discuss opportunities for new books, and greatly respected his advice. At this time Ken worked from a wooden garden shed behind his house at Knap Hill, High Wycombe, but he later removed to Swanage in Dorset where his attic was converted to a book room.

I anticipated the association going on for many years, but received a telephone call out of the blue, just before Christmas 1975, to say that the business was closing down. 'What do you mean, closing down?' was my immediate response. I was advised that Ken's doctor had said that he had to cease work straight away for reasons of health, and he was doing just that. 'But what about the business?' I asked. It seemed that he and his wife did not think that anyone else could take over and run the business, and were just literally going to shut up shop (or attic), sell off the books and put an end to it. A day or so later I went down to Swanage. Until that time I had no interest whatsoever in getting into retail bookselling but felt that I had to ensure the continuity of the Ken Trotman business, not only as an outlet for Arms & Armour Press, but because of the service it rendered the whole subject area. On one side of a sheet of paper we worked out the profile for the business, the sales and his valuation of the stock, and then we agreed a price. We were both very much stabbing at a fair figure for the other party, this not being a high-powered negotiation.

One aspect of transferring the business was the use of Ken's name. At the end of our discussion he and his wife asked, 'Well, Lionel, what are you going to call the business?' It hadn't occurred to me to change the existing name, and I said immediately that I wanted to continue calling it 'Ken Trotman'. From my viewpoint, his name was part of the asset value of the business. They questioned this, because they were such kind and modest people: 'But Ken will no longer be involved,' they said, to which I replied that I knew this but regarded his name as being like that of, say, Marks & Spencer, and as part of the label on the business. They were surprised, I think they were a little embarrassed, and were pleased. They said that it would be my decision, and they would be understanding if I wanted to change it, but that they were happy if I did continue to use it. In fact for many years afterwards visitors would ask for Ken Trotman, and when meeting Richard Brown would speak to him as either 'Ken' or 'Mr Trotman' and this continues to the present day.

A couple of weeks later I went down to Dorset with a colleague and loaded into the car Ken's book stock plus a plastic bag with some records, and a shoebox with index cards with the names and addresses of the customers, and we returned to London: we were the proud possessors of a business we had no idea how to run.

To find space close to our Arms & Armour Press offices we rented an empty office on the top floor of one of the buildings that also housed Ian Norrie's High Hill Bookshop, alongside our own offices, and the way to get to it was to go down the stairs from the publishing offices, cross the courtyard containing the dustbins from the supermarket, unlock the rear door to Norrie's shop, cut across his stock room and go up three flights of stairs.

To get the business underway we started sorting through Ken's business records, and found that effectively he had none. As he paid an invoice he jotted the details onto the cheque stub and threw away the invoice, and kept no other record – he knew where the books came from; we had no idea. Also he did not keep records of what he sold. Although he had passed to us an index file of about 2,000 names, there were no notes as to the interests of the people, what books they bought, or whether they bought anything at all. As they paid for books he paid the money into his bank account and kept no further record. Everything was in his head, but even this was fine as Ken had said that he would be available at the end of a telephone line and happy to help. However, just a couple of months after the transfer of the business, and whilst we were still working out exactly what was involved and before we had done anything to promote the firm, sadly he died. The doctor had been correct, and there was good reason for his having to stop work in the way that he did.

It was whilst we were understanding just what we had undertaken that I received a telephone call from his former partner, a Mr Chalmers Hallam. Over the years he had built up the business of books on fishing and hunting, and among the collections he had bought there were books on antique arms and armour. As the long-standing arrangement had been that Ken would not sell books on the sports aspects of things, the gentleman had reciprocated by not selling any of these books on antique arms and armour, but now he needed the space. He invited me down to his Ringwood home and showed me at the back of the garden a shed with thousands of books. 'How much will you give me for them?' he asked. I was flabbergasted. I knew that there were any number of treasures in there, but there was no way that I could put a value on such a range of books, and I wasn't at all sure about how Ken would have set about selling them. I explained this, but the dealer said that he had to clear the space and I should come up with a figure. I spent a couple of hours looking over the stock, and did so: a figure that was to me a low one, but necessarily realistic. 'It's a deal,' the dealer said, and I returned to London with a car stacked full, and laden down, with all the books. The Ken Trotman business therefore now had Ken's stock and this additional stock, and was ready to sell books if we but knew how.

The new business of course needed new staff and although we had a succession of juniors it was important to find an appropriate manager. We did so in Richard Brown. Richard worked at that time for Heffers of Cambridge, lived in Cambridge, was an experienced bookseller and also had a strong personal interest in military history. He undertook the daily commute from Cambridge for many years, until his eventual buy-out of the business. Richard set about increasing the stocks and sales of the Ken Trotman business, which multiplied many, many fold. We often questioned, with pleasure, what Ken Trotman himself would have said if he had returned and seen the development of his original enterprise. As the business grew, at one stage we called in a structural engineer to make sure that the stocks that were on the fourth floor above Ian Norrie's shop would stay there, and not descend to the ground floor!

Shortly after the relocation of the business a feature about it appeared in *Antique Arms and Militaria*, and reflecting the particular office space it occupied they wrote:

'One could be forgiven for thinking that a visit to Ken Trotman's mail-order bookshop in Hampstead should not be undertaken by those of a nervous disposition. Imagine it: here you are, at last, climbing the stairs of Arms & Armour Press's offices, having spent an exasperating thirty minutes pounding furiously up and down Hampstead High Street desperately searching for those elusive numbers 2–6! On arrival at Arms and Armour, you find that they are a sort of relay station. You are politely informed that a telephone call will be made and you will be escorted to what is rather disconcertingly called "the other side!" Your guide arrives! He/she takes you through a bewildering maze of corridors, doors and stairs, until K. Trotman is finally reached. Unless one is endowed with the instincts of a bloodhound, it is near-nigh impossible to find. By this time you are probably wondering whether it is worth it. Well, let me assure you that it is.'

At Herbert Jenkins.

Top: the team, summer 1964. Seated are Derek Grimsdick, and facing right Tom Eagle and left Lionel Leventhal. Behind Tom is Irving Farren, who subsequently joined Arms & Armour Press. Rosemary Atkinson is seated on the ground in front of Tom Eagle.

Right: J. Derek Grimsdick.

Left: The first offices in Childs Hill, 1969.

Below left: The building of 2-6 Hampstead High Street, 1970.

Right: Richard Brown with Lionel Leventhal in the Ken Trotman office in Hampstead High Street.

Below right: The team at Arms & Armour Press, 1980. Some key figures are (front row, left) Lynda Jones, (third left) Tony Evans, (centre) David Gibbons, and Lionel and Elizabeth Leventhal on the right. Second row, left is Richard Brown.

Left: At the Arm[?]
Fair, March 1968[?]

Below: The
village of
Kronberg, about
15 miles from
Frankfurt.

Above: Mark Wray with Dina and Eddie Coffey on the Greenhill stand at the Frankfurt Book Fair.

Right: Bill Corsa.

Above left: John Taylor.

Left: Greg Oviatt.

Above right: The Stackpole team at BookExpo America, 2000. (From left to right) Leigh Ann Berry, Dave Ritter, Donna Pope, Pat Moran, Mark Allison, Judith Schnell and Peter Rossi.

Right: James Opie.

The team at Greenhill Books. This photograph was taken at the celebration of Mark Wray's appointment to the Board in August 2000. From left to right, back row: Lionel Leventhal, Hugh Allan, Cath Stuart, Andrew Tarring, Sue McCormack, Mark Wray, Jonathan North and Jean Marc Evans. Seated from left

to right: Elizabeth Leventhal, Lynda Jones and Kate Ryle (who left to study as a barrister in September 2001). Not present, away on holiday, was Sue Cairncross. Since this photograph was taken, David Palmer and Judic Gendarme have joined the team.

Left: Robert L. Pigeon.

Below left: Colonel Robert and
Mrs. Edie Kane.

Right and below: Cecil Lewis
in World War One, and on the re-
publication of *Sagittarius Rising*
with Dr. Michael Fopp, Director of
the Royal Air Force Museum.

Left: Dr. David G. Chandler.

Below left: Ian Knight.

Below: John Walter.

Above: Ian Hogg.

Right: Chaim Herzog.

Left:
Jeffrey L. Ethell.

Below left:
John Elting.

Below:
Edward Ryan.

Right: Jack Gill.

Far right:
Kenneth Macksey.

Below right:
Paddy Griffith.

Above: Peter Tsouras.   **Below:** Sheila Watson and James Lucas

There is of course a world of difference between a business run single-handed by a man from his home, and one based in London with costly office overheads. These additional costs had been met by expanding the business: the book stock had been increased and mail-order service widened. We built up a stock which probably totalled something like 10,000 books on all military subjects. The range covered new and out-of-print books, second-hand, rare and antiquarian, with quite a few real treasures.

Because of the treasures on the shelves of Ken Trotman I had to cease my own collecting of books, because I felt it not practical to collect against myself and the Ken Trotman business, or to siphon books off. Fortunately I had already collected a number of key books and afterwards was able to find more. I am delighted to have on the shelves of my study classic works such as A. Essenwein's *Quellen zur Geschichte für Feuerwaffen*, Oswald Trapp & J. G. Mann's *The Armoury of the Castle of Churburg*, Guy Francis Laking's *A Record of European Arms and Armour* and *The Armour of Windsor Castle* (one copy being for royal presentation), Edwin J. Brett's *Pictorial Records of Arms & Armour*, Bashford Dean's *Catalogue of European Daggers* and *Catalogue of European Court Swords*, James Drummond and Joseph Anderson's *Ancient Scottish Weapons* and so forth to a wide range across military history from *The Perfection of Military Discipline* (London, at the Golden Ball, 1701) to the *Manual for Air Raid Warden Instruction* (Boston, Mass., 1942) and, as you might imagine, a number on the Napoleonic Wars.

It was during the time of the expansion of the Ken Trotman business that Arms & Armour Press was growing, and we published books such as *Who Dares Wins*. The Arms & Armour Press business employed nearly twenty people at that time, and was at the height of its success. I often had to sit in my office making decisions concerning considerable (in our publishing terms) sums of money, and matters of policy, and sometimes I felt that I was getting a little remote from actual books. It was therefore a particular pleasure for me to take time out, and go across to the Ken Trotman business, and meet individual customers dealing with individual books. Which, I questioned, was the real world?

In 1981 I encouraged Richard Brown to undertake some publishing, to restore specialist rare books to print. The first was *Journal of a Regimental Officer during the Recent Campaign in Portugal and Spain* by Peter Hawker. Over the years since then, quality limited editions have been published of over sixty rare titles, mostly original memoirs from the Napoleonic Wars but including some books on arms and armour, notably the monumental project of reprinting Guy Francis Laking's six-volume *Record of European Armour and Arms Through Seven Centuries* (the bible of studies of antique arms), with a new introduction by Claude Blair. I was happy to instigate this publishing for I very much feel that for specialist, niche subjects, the specialist niche bookseller (or for that matter the learned society) is closer to the audience than a trade publisher.

When I determined to sell the Arms & Armour Press the Ken Trotman business was kept separate from it, and discussion ensued with Richard Brown as to a management buy-out. As when I took over the Ken Trotman business from Ken himself, both Richard and I wanted to ensure the continuity of this important business for the specialist enthusiast and were able to make an arrangement that was practical to both sides. He agreed to take over the business and transfer it to his home town, Cambridge, into an old brewery which had been split up into work rooms. He did this early in 1985, and by that time he was married and had two young children. His wife Roz started helping him in the business, as did (in their own way) his two daughters.

Richard Brown has long experience of the Ken Trotman business and is probably the most knowledgeable bookman in the world upon many specialist subjects, or amongst the top few. There are a small number of booksellers of second-hand, rare and antiquarian books whom I have always recommended when consulted by those seeking books, and the names I provide may change according to particular need but invariably – for knowledge, service, trustworthiness and courtesy – the name of Richard Brown at Ken Trotman is always included.

We think Ken Trotman himself would be very proud if he returned and saw how the business he started fifty years ago has developed and grown, always maintaining his principles of knowledgeable service.

13

HOW THE LONDON BOOK
FAIR STARTED

IT WAS IN THE SPRING OF 1971 that I conceived the event that was held later in the year on 5 November 1971, the forerunner of the modern London Book Fair. In those days library book budgets were substantial, and the new generation of small publishers was beginning to feel that librarian buyers were not sufficiently aware of their publications. Librarians have always been inundated with all sorts of paperwork, catalogues and mailing shots from the big boys, and the small publishers were not getting the attention that they felt their lists deserved. I was keen to show, and sell if I could, my Arms & Armour Press books to librarians. In fact, one argument that I used was that small publishers often produce better books than the larger publishers, because of the individual and often specialist care and knowledge concentrated upon them. If the librarians actually saw the books then they could make an informed buying decision. So I had the idea of a small exhibition. I circulated a note about it to a number of similar small publishing houses saying, 'Let's put on a show.' And twenty-one other publishers agreed to join such an event.

The exhibition was held in the basement of the handsome Edwardian-built Berners Hotel, off London's Oxford Street. The location was chosen because of its proximity to the Library Association, and invitations were sent out to all public libraries in the Greater London catchment area. The date was fixed because it also saw the monthly Council Meeting of the Library Association, which would be bringing to London a number of important out-of-town librarians. The first event was given the rather long, but descriptive, name of 'The Specialist Publishers' Exhibition for Librarians', and we arranged for it to be opened by Ken Harrison, OBE, FLA, then City Librarian of Westminster. The event was a great success. More than 200 librarians attended, and when we checked the visitors' book afterwards and the libraries that were represented, we calculated that those responsible for a combined book budget of £4,500,000 had been present at the event.

As an aside, yesteryear the purchasing of books for the public library system was substantial, and the specialist library suppliers were major accounts for Arms & Armour Press, and, in the early days, Greenhill Books. Probably the top two or three accounts were library suppliers, and there were three or four others in the top ten. Over the years there has been pressure upon library book funds, and nowadays probably only one of the library suppliers appears among the top ten accounts. This saddens us, because the British public library system used to be a jewel in the crown of British culture; but policies have changed, and instead of libraries being homes of culture and learning, there is now increased emphasis on popular paperbacks and bestsellers (nowadays nearly 50 per cent of all library purchases are paperbacks). You may appreciate that this is not a policy with which we agree wholeheartedly.

Because over the early years our exhibition grew sharply, and changed name and venue, a number of people in the book trade think that they went to the first. The visitors' book for 5 November 1971 however shows that 95 per cent of the visitors were professional librarians. The publishers who exhibited at the first event were:

Adams & Dart	Frank Cass
The Architectural Press	Clematis Press
Arms & Armour Press	Leo Cooper
Autopress	Crosby Lockwood
Clive Bingley	Dawsons of Pall Mall
Blandford Press	Hugh Evelyn

The Folio Society	B. A. Seaby
Gregg International Publishers	Seeley, Service & Co
The Library Association	Thorsons Publishers
Lund Humphries Publishers	Valentine, Mitchell
Orbach & Chambers	H. F. & G. Witherby

Based on the success of this first event, I had decided to make it a regular one, but I needed additional expertise. So I invited Clive Bingley, then publishing textbooks on librarianship, to be my partner. He brought to the precursor of the London Book Fair knowledge about the library world, and also undertook the administrative activities necessary for the event.

After an early Summer outing to Manchester, which disclosed the considerable logistical problems of a non-London site for a one-day event, the next exhibition was held in November 1972 at the Bloomsbury Centre Hotel, with the name adjusted to become 'The Small and Specialist Publishers' Exhibition for Librarians', and there were forty-five exhibitors; and in 1973 the event moved to October, the name changed to 'SPEX 73: The Small and Specialist Publishers' Exhibition'. It leapt forward in terms of exhibitors to 120, and now took up the whole of the exhibition space available at the Bloomsbury Centre Hotel. It was 'opened' by the Minister for the Arts, Lord Eccles, and for the first time invitations went out to booksellers.

Lord Eccles took the opportunity to announce on behalf of the Government that there were no plans to introduce VAT on books. This was at that time a matter of concern to all involved in the book trade, and hence the announcement was most welcome. In 1984/5, however, there was renewed furore in the book trade that VAT was about to be imposed in the 1985 budget by the then Chancellor, Nigel Lawson. It didn't happen. Clive Bingley and I met Mr Lawson at the launch party for the 1985 or 1986 Fair, and he avowed that he had never had the remotest intention of putting VAT on books, but that he could hardly have announced the fact in advance of the 1985 budget, however concerned and up in arms the book trade was.

In 1974 the event was held early in October, close to the Frankfurt Book Fair, so that it enabled overseas visitors to come to London for SPEX 74 and then go on to Frankfurt. A leading American co-edition publisher, known to many British publishers, came and other publishers followed his lead. Joe Reiner of Outlet could heft a book in his hand and make a deal on the spot for the purchase of a whole edition. Reiner's visit was most timely, and coincided with the new interest of American publishers to buy British co-editions, and this led to some excellent business being done by the exhibitors. It certainly gave a strong commercial justification for the event. It was about that time that one exhibitor came rushing over to me to report that he had just sold a 1,500-copy co-edition to an American publisher. 'That's great,' I said. 'I'll pass the news on to *The Bookseller.*' 'You've missed the point,' he exclaimed. 'The real story is that I showed him material for this project in his office five months ago, and he declined it. Now that he's seen the finished book, he's forgotten entirely that he declined earlier, and we've been able to make a deal.' There is no doubt that seeing finished books in the right setting creates interest and sales.

For 1975 there were two changes: the name became 'SPEX 75: The London Book Fair', and the event moved to the Intercontinental Hotel in London's Park Lane, which continued to be the venue for the following year, when the number of exhibitors grew to 130. It was in these early years, when the event was held just prior to the Frankfurt Book Fair, that a special dinner was held at Clive Bingley's club, the Savile in Brook Street, for key overseas visitors. A number of Commonwealth countries were taking collective stands, and would send either the secretary of their Publishers' Association, or a representative of the whole trade, and Clive and I would invite them to dinner. The older

London clubs still have a unique atmosphere, and these were most enjoyable occasions. They also meant that when I travelled overseas, to Canada or Australia, although my Arms & Armour Press was a small publishing house, I received much kind and gracious hospitality, and it also led to special relationships with the book trade magazines in a number of countries.

During this period of considerable growth there was some liaison and occasional discussions with the Publishers Association. Many of the members of the PA exhibited at the event, and the secretariat of the PA knew about it and would come along; they supplied information about the Fair to overseas visitors, but there was no direct support for the event from the PA. In one of these early years I was invited to lunch by the then Secretary of the PA, and its President, and went along prepared to discuss some way to share the event with them, even perhaps enter into some sort of partnership, if they could offer official involvement and encouragement of the major British publishing houses to participate. The thoughts in my mind never surfaced, because we were told that, although Clive Bingley and I were nice folk, we were small publishers, we should continue to do our own thing, and the PA would be friendly, but they really didn't want to be troubled or have any involvement. Thus until the London Book Fair was eventually sold, in 1985, to a major international exhibitions company, it was the only significant book-publishing Fair in the world to be entirely privately owned and operated.

In 1977 we dropped 'SPEX' from the title; the number of exhibitors rose to 217, which caused us to outgrow the Intercontinental Hotel, and we moved for the following year to the 'Great Room' at Grosvenor House, and extended the event across two days. Again the number of exhibitors grew, this time to 315. We also experienced a remarkable problem: a sudden, freak heatwave. Those were the days of ridiculous trade unions dictates, and the hotel's management had not dared to put on the hotel's

You are cordially invited to

The Specialist Publishers' Exhibition for Librarians

Small and
Specialist Publishers Exhibition

SPEX 73

The London Book Fair — SPEX 76

The evolution of the London Book Fair, 1971-1984

air-conditioning system overnight. The temperature outside, at the beginning of October, was eighty degrees Fahrenheit but it was probably above ninety degrees inside. We received many complaints, and a very strong message was passed to the hotel management. The following year the weather was chill, but the management had the air-conditioning put on especially for us just before the event and throughout everyone froze.

One memory from that time was the cloud of suspiciously pungent herbal smoke over an overseas travel book publisher's stand.

There were some interesting experiences in terms of learning how people themselves learn how to use a book fair, react to signs directing them, and the exhibitors' view of their stands. The first year that we were at the Intercontinental one publisher, whose stand was positioned immediately as visitors entered the hall, came and complained bitterly. He said that the visitors were focusing on the middle distance as they came in, and everyone just walked past his stand. He demanded that the next year he be positioned in the centre of the hall, and we did as requested. The following year we waited to see what the exhibitor at the position by the entrance would say, and indeed he came over to us. 'Oh dear,' I thought, 'are we going to have a problem?' He had come over to thank us especially for being so good as to, in his words, place him 'in the best position in the hall', where everyone who came in passed his stand and saw what he was publishing.

We continued for two more years at Grosvenor House before implementing a major decision. It is surprising that an international centre like London has such inadequate trade-exhibition facilities; quite often it is the site management which tells the exhibition organisers when they may hold their event. Our Fair had pivoted for several years on the Frankfurt Book Fair, but Frankfurt announce their dates only two or three years in advance, whereas a reservation at Grosvenor House had to be made some four or five years in advance. One year the London Book Fair ran right up to the eve of the Frankfurt Book Fair, so that exhibitors at both Fairs had to leave London the very moment the Fair closed in order to hasten over with their books and dummies to Frankfurt. We feared that one year the dates would coincide directly, which would be disastrous; or that another year too wide a gap would fall between the London Book Fair and Frankfurt to enable overseas visitors to take in both.

We felt that London now warranted a Fair that would stand on its own two feet, and not be an appendage to another event. We believed also that the English-language publishing world could accommodate two book fairs a year, one in the Spring and one in the Autumn, to facilitate the liaisons that were increasingly necessary, and the interchange of information. So we took the policy decision to move the London Book Fair to the Spring. To position the event in the Spring, we either had to move from October 1980 to the Spring of 1981 (which we reckoned was too short an interval), or to hold the event over for eighteen months, to April 1982 (which carried some risk of momentum-loss). We held the event over, and the response from the trade was extremely positive. The number of exhibitors at the 1980 event had been 330; this jumped to 508 for our first year at the Barbican in the City of London.

The first event was organised by me, on an ad hoc basis. The second too. But when it was apparent that the Fair would be an annual event, a more durable organisational framework became necessary. The location had to be chosen and reserved, committing us to a given size, and the required number of exhibiting publishers had to be secured. Sizes and layout of the table-top 'stands' had to be determined, some variations permitted, and in due course we entered upon the construction of display-stands, with titles and logos and the provision of shelving. Development was exhibitor-driven initially, but the prospective visitor-profile took on increasing importance as we sought to broaden the appeal of the Fair, and publicity depended on trade journals such as *The Bookseller*, *Publisher's Weekly* (USA), *Quill and Quire* (Canada), the *Australian Bookseller and Publisher*, and others, as well as liaison with the trade associations of Europe and the English-speaking world. By the time the venue shifted to Grosvenor House, a fully professional planning and administration system was in place. A full-time staff of (at first) three, including the director, grew to four or five, was aided by further in-house staff for the three months leading up to the Fair, and then by another twenty or more on-site for the Fair itself. Most of the latter were regulars each year, which made for smooth on-site procedures and generated a warm team-spirit in the somewhat bleak wastelands of the Barbican Centre. At the top of this staff-pyramid, Clive and I, with the director, ran the strategy, the financial management and the promotion and publicity; sales, site-planning and events, and other 'housekeeping' kept the permanent staff fully occupied twelve months of the year.

The Fair's major area of growth, which attracted significantly more exhibitors during the late 1970s and early 1980s, was in visitors from overseas, to a virtually complete conspectus of the international book trade with which British publishers worked. They included publishers who sought rights or co-editions in the English language, as well as publishers buying licences of English-language books for translation into their own languages. Many booksellers, and especially the agents and distributors who sold English-language books around the globe, were also included. Many of the Commonwealth countries were now sending collective exhibits and delegations. All of this led to complaints from visitors, which were repeated year after year, often in letters to *The Bookseller*: 'Where are the major UK publishers?' Although hundreds of publishers exhibited, most of the leading houses that dominated the general book trade turned up their noses. Yet they nevertheless expected the visitors to the Fair to break their journeys to go to the offices. Clive Bingley and I had a variety of reasons put to us for their non-participation, such as alleged doubts 'whether the Book Fair is a rights fair or a trade fair'; we replied that it was for anybody who wanted to do what business he desired in the book trade. A number of the houses said they 'had nothing to learn from a British book fair', because they knew about the sale of books already, were in touch with everyone that they needed to know, and they 'knew' that if they exhibited no new business would result. However, although these publishers would not take exhibition space, they still sent along editorial, rights and sales staff, to meet the Fair's visitors clandestinely, so to speak. We were able to track how many people came from which various publishing houses by means of our registration system. One year, amongst non-exhibitors, the Longman Group sent thirty-seven people, Collins twenty-six, Octopus eighteen, and Penguin fifteen. We thought it ironic that staff from these great houses had to come along with briefcases, and wander about the corridors to find their customers or partners, and then take them away for coffee to discuss their business, because their masters would not pay for a stand that served, they said, no useful purpose.

At the move of the event to the Barbican it took another leap forward in numbers of both exhibitors and visitors, but the Barbican was not a popular venue. We had been able to secure a reservation for it before building was quite complete, and were one of the earliest trade fairs to use the site. Its facilities were quite a shock. Firstly, the whole Barbican area was very badly signposted and people experienced considerable difficulties in locating the exhibition halls (I remember one person arriving in an hysterical state, who had been lost for nearly an hour). Secondly, the exhibition halls were very strange shapes, and had low ceilings. The reason for this (which we preferred not to publicise) was that the halls were originally planned to be car-parks. When, however, the City authorities discovered the enormous running costs of the Barbican, they sought a source of revenue by switching the space designated for car-parks to use for exhibitions.

Once installed at the Barbican the event seemed to reach a plateau. Although the number of overseas visitors increased, and the event was increasingly visible on the international scene, the number of exhibitors stabilised to:

1982	1983	1984	1985
508	497	510	520

It was this plateau of exhibitors that made Clive Bingley and me receptive to the approach (for the second time) from Industrial & Trade Fairs Limited, part of Reed International, to take over the event. We felt that if it was to move forward it needed to break with the perception of being run by two independent publishers (that ownership might have been one reason why the major publishing houses felt they had nothing to gain from the event), and new thinking, as well as long-term investment, was needed. At that time, the annual cost of running the event, hiring the exhibition facility, and so forth, totalled more than £300,000. Also, I have to say, the cash offered was encouraging.

Clive Bingley and I sold the London Book Fair shortly after the 1985 event. Industrial & Trade Fairs Limited immediately started to implement a plan for major growth, but were locked in to the Barbican for the 1986 event (which had 509 exhibitors). For 1987 they took the major step of moving the Fair to Olympia, and the subsequent enormous growth and success of the event over the years since then reflect their investment and their style of doing things (which swiftly persuaded, or provided an excuse for, the major publishers to support the Fair).

For many years the British Government, through its various export promotion schemes, supported British publishers going to Frankfurt and other international Fairs. Sometimes publishers exhibiting overseas have been fully subsidised, sometimes there has been a scale of subsidies. If only, however, in my period of involvement with the London Book Fair, there had been some means of aid to promote the Fair internationally, or bring into Britain key purchasers of British books, or potential purchasers, who can say to what size the Fair today would have grown, helping to secure the international markets for British books?

One question that has been repeatedly posed over the years is whether the public should be allowed in. The answer is, 'Yes, but they have been invited, but haven't come in any numbers.' Starting in the early 1980s there were announcements about the event, and indeed discounted tickets were offered by a number of magazines. The public response was desultory; although they would have been welcomed if they had come in significant numbers (and extra time could have been added so as to separate the public from the trade customers), there never was any great amount of public interest.

The London Book Fair has developed enormously since the mid-1980s. At that time one could personally know the great majority of the exhibitors, and also a significant percentage of the visitors. With growth, however, the event has gone forward to a much larger, higher level. It has been, perhaps, somewhat like watching a teenager grow up and exceed the parents' expectations, and the parent feels great pride in what their youngster is doing. I certainly had no idea at the outset that what I started in 1971 would become a major event of such value to the British and international book trades as the London Book Fair is today.

14

ABA, BEA AND MILITARY BOOK SHOW

MEETING DARTH VADER IN SAN FRANCISCO, having to watch nearly naked young ladies at a swimming pool over lunch in Las Vegas, and being chased by a rights person along an aisle in New York's Javits Convention Center: these are just some of the memories of more than twenty-five years of attending the ABA in the United States.

The early 1970s were a traumatic time for the British economy, and this impacted fiercely on the book trade, which had been simultaneously struck by an anti-trust suit brought by America's Federal Justice Department against US publishers who were buying and selling rights with British publishers. Something new and positive, however, coincided with this struggle: the now famous, focal point of the international book trade – the ABA (American Booksellers Association Convention and Exhibition, recently retitled BookExpo America) – moved to New York in 1975, and became both visible and accessible. I attended the event, and also wrote the first ever report about it for *The Bookseller*.

From time immemorial the ABA had been held at the Shoreham Hotel in Washington DC, for American booksellers only, but for its seventy-fifth anniversary it moved to New York. The event was presented in two hotels in close proximity, the Hilton and the Americana on New York's Avenue of the Americas (known locally as Sixth Avenue). The facilities of the hotels were really quite inadequate for book exhibits, and many of the stands were in remote and dark places within the buildings. This was in fact the last time the event was ever held in hotels; for good reason the ABA was held thereafter in exhibition halls, vast and ever vaster.

A small number of British publishers, myself included, took advantage of the event being held in New York to visit it. We found a window on the American book trade.

The trauma the British economy was facing at this time was inflation, and the special impact this had on the book trade – the effect of the different rates of inflation between Britain and America – was to place the cost of British books on the edge of impracticality over there, so eroding the major British export market. I reported in *The Bookseller* comments such as:

'British prices are becoming impossible,' said Milton Gladstone of Arco. 'Last year we imported about 70 books, but this year it will be down to maybe 10 to 15 and some of these were negotiated some time ago. In some cases prices have doubled in a year. We are now offering to produce from film supplied.' And he added: 'British books are being priced out of the market here. Your inflation of 30 per cent is way beyond ours of about 4 per cent in book prices.'

The other and very significant problem was the 'double whammy' effect of the hideously high inflation not being discounted by a declining sterling. When sterling weakened against the dollar, at one extreme point to just over $2.50/£1, this created all sorts of additional problems (obtaining books by indirect, unofficial channels) and infringement of copyright.

In using the ABA as a window on the American book trade, it could be seen that the size and wealth of the American market, then as now, was staggering. One of the adages that I have used over the years is to say that if a wall was built around Great Britain and we were no longer able to export, especially to the United States, the next day the great majority of British publishers would be out of business.

Again, quoting from the article in *The Bookseller:*

'All may not be perfect in the United States but their positive approach to publishing and selling comes, as one British publisher visiting the convention said, "as a refreshing breeze after the current stagnation and gloom in Britain." If the book world still revolves around Frankfurt for international rights, the largest and most vibrant book *market* is certainly the ABA convention.'

Following my report the Publishers Association was able to apply to the Board of Trade under a scheme whereby British companies exhibiting at an overseas fair received a subsidy. This led to a number of British publishers being able to exhibit for the first time ever at the ABA in the following year in Chicago, an arrangement that continues to this day. It was the next year, 1977, when the event was in San Francisco, that there was a major leap forward in terms of the number of visitors from outside the United States. San Francisco was the event, and place, that the international book trade had been waiting for (an opportunity to visit that charming and special city, on business expenses). About thirty British publishers had visited when the ABA was in New York; two years later it grew to over 100 visitors from elsewhere around the world. The number of exhibits also grew, from 350 to 450. It was at San Francisco that, as I wrote in *The Bookseller*, 'On the Ballantine stand there stood the seven-foot black-coated figure of Darth Vader, villain of the new S.F. novel *Star Wars*, just released and now a sensationally successful film.' The film was not to be released in Britain for some while, and I believe that this (my claim to fame) was the first ever reference to it in the British press.

The trend also began at that time for British publishers to set up distribution in the United States, and in my *Bookseller* article I interviewed these first pioneers, and I was myself led to follow a few years later (interviewing for *The Bookseller* providing me with much useful background, even intelligence).

Because the ABA is, as its name suggests, run by (until recently), and certainly for, the members of the American Booksellers Association, with all sorts of events and seminars linked to it, it has moved around the United States to facilitate ease of visiting by member booksellers in the main areas of the continent. I have kept a record of the event (every so often one wants to check back as to where one met somebody, or such comes up in conversation), and in my years it has moved around as follows:

1975	New York	1985	San Francisco	1995	Chicago
1976	Chicago	1986	New Orleans	1996	Chicago
1977	San Francisco	1987	Washington	1997	Chicago
1978	Atlanta	1988	Anaheim	1998	Chicago
1979	Los Angeles	1989	Washington	1999	Los Angeles
1980	Atlanta	1990	Las Vegas	2000	Chicago
1981	Chicago	1991	New York	2001	Chicago
1982	Anaheim	1992	Anaheim	2002	New York
1983	Dallas	1993	Miami		
1984	Washington	1994	Los Angeles		

Every year is memorable, usually for a different reason. The 1977 ABA in San Francisco was notable for me because of the many attractions of that city, but especially because I met Colonel Robert V. Kane for the first time. He had recently started Presidio Press, the most consistent American publisher solely devoted to quality military books over the years. He held a reception at the Presidio, and one of the guests there was a lonely, then unknown, Tom Clancy.

The 1980 ABA in Atlanta was memorable because it took me for the second time to Atlanta, and enabled me to visit the world famous Emery Medical Center. At that time videos were just starting as a form of mass entertainment, and I believed that they would have a good part to play in the world of reference, information and education. I undertook a survey as to what sort of videos were available in the United States, because it would be much easier to launch a video line for Britain and Europe if one was working from available material, rather than having to undertake the filming and production. One area that seemed to me to offer significant potential was the medical field, and Emery had produced a very important series of tapes showing leading surgeons undertaking operations. My idea was to bring these over to Britain, and make them available on the British video tape system for British doctors. I trusted Emery's capabilities, but visited them to further the negotiations where a licence was concerned. I did so after lunch one day, and such was their pride as to how they had furthered the filming of operations that they took me into their private viewing cinema to show me the excellence of their filming, how every detail was shown, and how they had managed intimate close-ups of the surgeon at work. This was just what I did not need after an excellent lunch. Somehow I managed to stick it out, but was not rewarded because when 'Leventhal Medical Video' undertook test marketing and a viewing of sample video tapes at the British Medical Association, there was minimal response.

With the event moving in 1984 to Washington DC, I conceived the idea of another event in order to give credibility and encouragement to military publishing in the United States. At that time the United States was still in post-Vietnam trauma, and anything military was an anathema. There was abhorrence of military books by bookshops, and I felt that a positive way of promoting the subject area was by having a showcase.

I suggested the idea to a number of the publishers with whom I then worked with my Arms & Armour Press, and they were encouraging and offered support. They offered support, that is, if somebody else would take on making all the arrangements. This I did, and based the event on experience gained from running the London Book Fair and other promotions.

It was decided to have the event on the day before the ABA was held, because that would mean that many publishers, especially those from Britain, would be in the capital at that time and would therefore be available to man their stand and have, one hoped, useful and beneficial discussions with the visitors. We were fortunate, by kind courtesy of Norman Polmar, in being able to obtain the conference rooms at the National Press Club. It was to be a table-top event, and I arranged things so that the cost for exhibiting was kept to a minimum, but each publisher had to make some sort of contribution to running the event. So, for example, one publisher undertook the printing of the invitations, another undertook the general mailing, and so forth. During the set-up period for the event itself I organised who would man the reception desk, and the various details of making the show run smoothly.

That first event was an enormous success. The room was packed out, with keen visitors ranging from defence attaches, to military librarians, plus, of course, authors and trade visitors. Following its great success it was decided to continue with the Military Book Show, but I stepped aside from running it, and it was agreed that when the event was on the Eastern Seaboard it would be run by the Naval Institute Press (Jim Sutton), and on the West Coast by Presidio (Richard Kane). When the event was held half way between the two it went to whoever held their hand up first.

One memorable event was in New York in 1991 when the show was held on the aircraft carrier *Intrepid*. This historic ship is permanently moored as a museum. The day was swelteringly hot, and the ship was not air-conditioned. At one stage I was having a conversation with an author and we moved into the open at the aft of the ship (the fan tail), where it had started to rain gently . Another event, that in Miami in 1973, was held at an unfortunately remote location. Having the event at the Miami aquarium may have sounded a good idea, but it was too far for visitors to get to. Also it was remarkably warm, once again, and astonishingly humid. The event was held out of doors, under an open sided tent, and as the hours of the exhibition went by one could watch the bindings of books warp.

In 1999 the management of the Military Book Show was handed on to Primedia Enthusiast Publications History Group, whose publications include *Military History*, *MHQ: The Quarterly Journal of Military History*, and *Civil War Times Illustrated*. One benefit this new management has brought to the event is that it is now advertised in their magazines, and thus for the first time there were non-trade visitors, people with a serious interest in military history and books. Their number contributed to the busy atmosphere of the event. Yes, it was good to sell books, but for this event publishers only bring a single copy for trade exhibit. A number of these visitors stayed on until the middle of the afternoon when publishers were happy to sell books; Greenhill participated 'care of' our US distributors Stackpole Books (who then also distributed Osprey), and one visitor bought seventeen of the Osprey books.

For 2002 the show returns to New York and the *Intrepid*, and Jim Sutton returns to the promotion of it.

Continuing with the memories of the ABA, 1986 in New Orleans was memorable only for being one of the quietest ABAs, with fewer visitors than ever before. This is because New Orleans itself is not a significantly populated city, and there was no centre of such within a considerable distance. Hence ABA only appealed to those who would fly from either coast. It was hot and steamy, and a great pleasure to stroll around the French Quarter in the cool of the evening, in short sleeves, and listening to jazz. It seemed as though the exhibition hall emptied itself into the French Quarter, and one could stroll around in the evening meeting socially those folk whom one had been in conversation with during the daytime.

At the Las Vegas ABA in 1990 many publishers took affront at the book trade, representing culture, being on show in the world centre of gambling. It seemed that all who went swore off gambling, but surprisingly those who spoke about gambling were the ones who had won.

The 1991 ABA was valuable to me because, as I was walking along a gangway, somebody ran after me and called my name. It was the rights assistant from Henry Holt, whom I had met some years ago at another publisher. I confess that I had forgotten her, but she remembered me and had dashed along the gangway to show me that Henry Holt was publishing *The Illustrated Napoleon* by David Chandler. That chance encounter with a sprinting rights person led to Greenhill undertaking the publication of the book.

The moving of the event around the United States enabled me and my wife to tour quite a lot of the continent. A pattern developed whereby I would work for four or five days in New York, and then would head off the weekend before the ABA in the direction of the event but tour on the way and finish up in the city where the ABA was to be held. For example in 1977 we flew from New York to Las Vegas, and saw the Grand Canyon, had a wonderful drive through Death Valley and up to the Yosemite, to arrive in San Francisco in time for the ABA. Afterwards we were able to drive down Route 1 to fly out of Los Angeles. Another memorable trip was when, in order to get to the ABA in Anaheim, we flew to Denver, toured Colorado, drove down through New Mexico to Santa Fe, and then flew the rest of the way. These tours continued for a period of seven or eight years, and enabled us to see more of the United States than some Americans have.

One benefit of the ABA is that many publishers stack heaps of complimentary copies of their forthcoming books, usually as large-format paperbacks, for ABA visitors to take away and read. They hope that this starts 'word of mouth' recommendation, and especially that booksellers will talk about the good books that they have read in advance of publication. I have always been very happy to help myself to these heaps, and there is usually a rush first thing in the morning for the most attractive books (it must be somewhat disappointing for some publishers whose heaps are ignored). I have usually managed to bring back a dozen or fifteen books, which become my summertime leisure reading.

One of the major downsides however of the ABA is that the convention facilities usually have appalling catering (and in the first year of its recent return to Chicago there was no catering at all). Over the years I've worked out several ways around this. One is to check the area near one's hotel to see if there is a good deli, and if so to take a packed lunch in with one. I've sometimes entertained by means of taking in a couple of packed lunches, with accoutrements and dessert, and then had to find somewhere in the exhibition facility to picnic. Another way is to encircle the block of the convention facility to see if there is anywhere nearby where one can eat. Over the years I've found some interesting and good places. One such year was in Washington DC when I discovered if one left by the rear entrance to the exhibition facility one was just across the road from the Smithsonian Museum of American Art. The first day a couple of friends and I used their cafeteria. Each of us seems to have told other people, for the next day it was half full, and for the third day it was totally jammed with conventioneers. However, the ABA is sometimes held over the Memorial Day weekend, as it was on this particular occasion, when the Museum does not expect people to come for lunch, and this caused severe congestion, shortages and so forth. Hence when the event returned to Washington DC a couple of years later and I went back for lunch on the first day I mentioned the situation to the manager, and there was excellent catering throughout the holiday period. However on the last day, as my colleagues and I were leaving to return to the ABA, a lady volunteer who was in charge of the entrance got up and stood in front of us not permitting us to leave. 'Gentlemen,' she said, 'I've seen you come in every day, walk straight past the exhibits, go and eat, and then walk out again. Do you realise what a wonderful museum this is?'

We demurred somewhat, saying that we were enjoying walking through the Museum to the cafeteria, but we had business to do. 'No,' she said, 'you must spend five minutes with me viewing our museum' and with that she took us in tow, and gave us a quick tour, and then sent us on our way.

Las Vegas was also memorable for one particular lunchtime meeting. A Canadian publisher and I sat in the sun and in our business suits, by the swimming pool at Caesar's Palace. My friend, Bill Hanna, was between the pool and me, so that I was able to sit watching the nearly naked young ladies diving and swimming. I forget what we ate, or if any business resulted.

As the event has grown into one of America's largest trade conventions, there have been few enough cities with the combination of the right size of exhibition facility and hotel and restaurant infrastructure to accommodate the many thousands who attend. Hence in 1995 it was decided to have the event on a permanent basis centrally in the United States in Chicago. Perhaps because in the first year the facilities in Chicago were in a state of collapse, there was an outcry from booksellers on both coasts (and many publishers), and this led to the 1999 BEA being in Los Angeles, 2002 in New York, and the pattern for the coming years has now been scheduled to be:

30 May – 1 June 2003:	Los Angeles
4–6 June 2004:	Chicago
3–5 June 2005:	New York

BookExpo America is the window on the world of American general trade publishing, and always stimulating and exciting.

15

HAVING A NUMBER ONE BESTSELLER

IT IS RARE – IN FACT PROBABLY UNIQUE – for a specialist military publisher to have a number one bestseller. This happened to me in the summer of 1980 with Tony Geraghty's *Who Dares Wins*.

When I commissioned the book few people had heard about the SAS. Indeed, telling a colleague that we had done so made him query whether the Arms & Armour Press list was now going to publish books on civil aviation, for the only SAS in general parlance at that time was the Scandinavian airline.

The very talented author of the book, Tony Geraghty, was the ideal man to undertake the project. He was the Defence Editor for the London *Sunday Times* and hence, on the one hand, was at the top of the military journalism profession, and, on the other, he knew members of the SAS and went sport parachuting with them.

As Tony was writing the book there was a power struggle between the owner of the newspaper and the print unions, which led to the newspaper being shut down for what became a period of ten months. All the journalists were kept on, on full salary, and many took advantage to write articles for other papers, find ways to double their salaries, or to take interesting facility trips to far-away places. Not Tony. When we received draft (and excellent) chapters from him it was apparent that he was working full-time on the project. We met and I said to him 'Tony, what you are doing is really fine, but no-one has heard about the SAS and as a specialist book the audience will be limited. We estimate a print run of 3,500 copies and you really ought to consider whether you should be working full-time on it; you are effectively subsidising it.' 'Yes,' he responded, 'I know, and I've done the arithmetic. But I know the people, and I want to do a good book for them.'

When it became time to discuss what to call the book I favoured something like *The Story of the SAS*. Tony favoured using the motto of the regiment, *Who Dares Wins,* with explanatory sub-title. 'That sounds good,' I said, 'but nobody knows the expression. It means nothing.' Tony was keen on it, however, and so I went along with it.

We started our work on the production of the book and the arrival of proofs coincided with the memorable day when an event took place that would shoot the SAS to international fame: terrorists took over the Iranian Embassy in London.

There was, however, no immediate connection with the SAS. The siege continued for several days, starting in the middle of the week and then running through the weekend. It attracted enormous and international publicity, which was probably what the terrorists wanted, and there was a large encampment of the world's media in Hyde Park facing the embassy at Palace Gate, Kensington. Over the weekend I suddenly remembered that we were distributing a book from an American publisher entitled *Police Tactics in Armed Situations* and I realised that what we should have done was to send someone down to the press encampment with a couple of dozen copies, and sell them to the media people. We would therefore have made some sales but also the book would probably have received some publicity. Hence it was with enormous disappointment that I switched on the television at about six o'clock in the evening before the office re-opened (it was the Spring Bank Holiday weekend) and saw live the attack on the embassy. 'What a pity,' I thought, as I watched the black-clad figures abseil down the front of the building, 'there goes the sale of *Police Tactics in Armed Operations.*'

It was only as the news was expanded upon that it became apparent that those who had attacked the embassy were the SAS. That whole evening there was more and more about the SAS on all the television channels. In fact there was an avalanche of news and information, much ill-informed, about the SAS over the next day or two.

We announced *Who Dares Wins*, Tony's choice for the book title having suddenly become the most famous motto in the world. There was an immediate auction for the newspaper rights, which sold for a five-figure sum to the *Daily Mail*, and I also auctioned, pre-publication, the paperback rights. Fontana won and the book has been continuously in print since then. The BBC TV series *Panorama* wanted us to delay publication so as to enable a programme to be made to coincide; we were in the astonishing, privileged position of being ahead of the entire world with information about the SAS, and hence we declined and they had to hasten their plans.

We slightly delayed passing the book for press, to allow Tony to include coverage about the Iranian Embassy siege, but we were the only people with an inside, quality book about the SAS, and when it was published the sales took off like a rocket. We had exceptional coverage in the press and, overall, we sold 100,000 copies in hardback. That would of course have been exceptional for a general trade publisher, but it must be unique where a specialist publisher is concerned.

Every business has to have its accounts audited every year, and so too with publishing houses. We would have a team of three or four audit clerks come into our offices, and I always encouraged them to query things, and say if they had found a better system, or a different way of doing things, in another business. Sometimes one picks up useful hints that way. The year of *Who Dares Wins*, one of the audit clerks came to me, shaking his head. 'Why did you publish any others books this year, Mr Leventhal?' he queried. 'You only needed to have published one book, the book *Who Dares Wins*.' I gently had to tell him that if publishers knew which book was going to be a bestseller then he would be quite right, and they would indeed only publish a single book.

Tony told me one story (which I hope is not an SAS myth) that is not in the book. The SAS were trained in HALO parachuting (HALO meaning High Altitude, Low Opening) which calls for jumping out of an aeroplane at a great height, and delaying opening a parachute for as long as possible. The SAS pioneered HALO for military purposes, although now free fall parachuting has become something of a sport. In developing the military capabilities, they also created special jump-suits to facilitate their jumping from a considerable height, which entailed having an enclosed helmet and an oxygen supply, and being able to manoeuvre and track across country a considerable distance, which called for a jump-suit with aerodynamic capabilities, fins and so forth.

The event that Tony told me about concerned a small unit of SAS who jumped on an exercise over Southern England one dark, overcast night. For some reason I cannot recall they totally missed their drop zone on Salisbury Plain, and in tracking across country lost their bearings entirely and came to ground miles upon miles from where they should be. I guess that's what training is all about. They had no idea where they were, and seeing a distant and remote farmhouse they walked to it through the countryside in the dead of night, and banged upon the door. There was a wait, and then noises within and a light went on. The front door creaked open and there stood a little old lady. 'Madam, we are lost. Can you please tell us where we are?' they politely asked. She looked upon them with horror, cried 'Earth!' and slammed the door.

Who Dares Wins really is a case of quality, and virtue, being rewarded. The quality of the book was due to Tony Geraghty's knowledge and professionalism, and the virtue was his concentrating on the book when he could easily have been doing something else.

Following *Who Dares Wins* I published at Arms & Armour Press a succession of successful books about Special Forces including Tony Geraghty's *Inside the SAS*, James Ladd's *SBS: The Invisible Raiders* and Peter Dickens' *SAS: The Jungle Frontier*. Dickens' book was launched at a very special reception at the Special Forces Club, behind Harrods. Because members of the SAS are on secondment from various regiments, they usually serve their term with the SAS and go back to their regiments, and it may be a number of years before, if ever, they meet again. For Peter Dickens' extremely well-written book about the Borneo campaign the unit which took part in this was reassembled, and its members met for the first time in many years. It was a wonderful friendly gathering, with a divide between the men who fought in Borneo and the handful of book trade people that I had invited. Again, unusually for a launch party, there was an express 'no publicity' demand. When the representative of *The Bookseller* produced a camera the room suddenly started emptying. The desirability of having a photograph in order to promote the book in the book trade magazine was discussed, and there was a careful check as to whose picture could appear and whose could not. There was a sorting process, and finally a group was put together and a photograph taken.

Another special book by a special man, a very much larger-than-life figure, was *Delta Force* by Charlie Beckwith. In the children's comic *Beano* there is a cartoon character called Desperate Dan, who in preference to opening a door would walk straight through it. Charlie Beckwith was like that, and he came over for the launch of the book and an exhausting author tour. The book was very successful, and Charlie Beckwith certainly survived walking through a very demanding door – the formidable tour – but we were all totally shattered.

My interest in publishing about Special Forces continues, and Greenhill has published a number of books about the SAS and restored other books on Special Forces to print.

16

THE ONE
THAT GOT AWAY

THE DECISION-TAKING about the books that are to be published is akin to the Greek art of divination by haruspication: go to the remainder shops and see the books for which the publishers once had high hopes (and sometimes made significant investment). Some you win; some you lose. One book I let pass was *The Hunt for Red October*, the first, best-selling novel by Tom Clancy.

In 1984 *The Hunt for Red October* was being prepared for publication by the Naval Institute Press, Annapolis, who have the world's leading publishing programme of naval books. I started working with them on a co-edition basis in the 1970s, the first book published with them being *British Battleships of the Second World War* by Alan Raven and John Roberts, followed by books such as *The German Navy in World War II* by Jak Mallman Showell, *The Warships of the Imperial Japanese Fleet* by Hansgeorge Jentschura, Dieter Jung and Peter Mickel, *British Cruisers of the Second World War* by Alan Raven and John Roberts, and many other fine books in a special landscape format. In return Arms & Armour Press took Naval Institute Press books on a co-edition basis, and then set up the distribution of the whole Naval Institute Press publishing programme for Britain, Europe and the Commonwealth. Hence due to our close relationship we were the first British, indeed international, publisher to be offered rights in *The Hunt for Red October*. I chose to decline.

The Naval Institute Press were publishing the book as a way to get American submariners, during the Cold War, interested in submarine warfare, and when they started their work on it had planned a first print run of only 2,000 or 3,000 copies.

At the time when the book was offered, early spring 1984, Arms & Armour Press was at a high point of success. We had published *Who Dares Wins* and a series of very successful books about special forces followed soon after. As a consequence (and the main reason for rejection), the Arms & Armour Press sales team were at full stretch and I did not want to divert them to see another, different, buyer in the shops that they visited, because fiction buying is handled by a different person from the buyer for the military and general sections. Such extra and special work for just a single book would not be worth the time involved. I also have to say that I thought that the book, which had already had extensive editorial work done on it, needed further cutting in the middle. I did, however, think that the book could be published by a publishing house that regularly published fiction, and as part of our friendly relationship with the Naval Institute Press we advised on the sale of the UK rights, to Collins.

Sales of *The Hunt for Red October* did not take off following publication, on either side of the Atlantic, for quite a while. It was not until President Reagan, some months later (the following February) recommended the book that it began to receive wide attention, and the Naval Institute Press's marketing director Jim Sutton undertook a very successful marketing campaign.

The close relationship enjoyed with the Naval Institute Press led in the early 1980s to another very special co-edition. I had dinner one evening in Kronberg, Frankfurt at the time of the Book Fair, with the then Press Director Tom Epley. We were talking about our sons. Kevin Epley was eleven years old and Michael Leventhal ten. 'How about a co-edition of sons?' I suggested, meaning that we would exchange them. We both thought that it was a great idea and went home to tell our wives, who did not. They both questioned the wisdom of sending a boy of that age across the Atlantic to stay with a family he had never met. However, the following summer Kevin came and stayed with the Leventhal family in Elstree, Hertfordshire. He was a great natural sportsman, soon learned and was great at cricket, and the year after Michael went to Annapolis.

As part of the close relationship with the Naval Institute Press, when they offered us a fine reference work *Secretaries of the Navy*, we responded with a synopsis offering the companion book *Secretaries of the British Navy*. Theirs was about high office in the US Government; ours provided information about the training of secretaries, typing speeds, cut-away diagrams of typewriters, and an appendix listing officers they served under.

Digressing somewhat, but having mentioned publishing the important naval reference work *British Battleships of the Second World War*, this book gave me a particular lesson in finance, cash flow and the reality of money. When one is assessing the investment in a book it is an arithmetic exercise, and one reviews the costs, mark-up, capital commitment, and cash flow. In this particular case, at the time that this very substantial book was being undertaken, it was the largest ever project that I had had. I forget the amount of money involved, but think it was something like £40,000 (at that time something above $75,000). The day on which I signed the production investment schedule committing us was also the day on which I reached home to find my wife somewhat upset. The reason for this was that as Elizabeth had come out of the supermarket and loaded the car with her shopping she had dropped a package containing a jar of mayonnaise and it had shattered. She was very upset because this was the loss of 40 pence. The 40-pence loss was however in the real world, cash out of one's own purse (or pocket), whereas the £40,000 investment was all on paper.

Meanwhile, reverting to *The Hunt for Red October*, in charge of rights at the Naval Institute Press was Debbie Grosvenor, who orchestrated the sale of the book to many countries. Translation rights were licensed to twenty countries in all, and of course there was also the very popular film with Sean Connery. The Naval Institute Press have now sold half a million copies of the book in hardback (yes, that's in hardback), and it continues to sell at 5,000 copies a year. What a phenomenon!

Tom Clancy went on to fame and fortune following the publication of *The Hunt for Red October*, and the sales of his books now total above 100 million copies, with many of them filmed. I understand that early copies of his books now sell for substantial sums, more so for early proof copies. Mine, however, was thrown out as soon as the rights were sold to Collins.

It was always a pleasure to visit the Naval Institute Press, for their handsome offices were in the grounds of the Naval Academy in Annapolis, Maryland, the college for America's naval officers, a short walk from the historic and attractive town. A few years ago, however, they moved into their own new building just off the campus.

And, yes, I still think the decision to turn *The Hunt for Red October* down was the right one for my Arms & Armour Press at that time.

17

GREENHILL BOOKS:
THE FIRST DECADE

GREENHILL BOOKS TODAY has come a long way from its origins in October 1984, in the Arms & Armour Press offices in Hampstead. In the period leading to my sale of Arms & Armour Press, there had been a significant development in printing: the short-run printing process. A combination of factors enabled a British printer, Anthony Rowe, to set up a system whereby books could be printed economically in lower quantities than ever before. A short run meant that one could reprint books that were out of stock, or reprint older titles that were out of print but catered for niche or specialist audiences, in a publishing context. Nowadays 'on demand' printing is a practicality, but this is different from being able to publish an edition of a book economically in a low quantity. I started discussions concerning setting up a system to reissue military books that were 'in demand', the original intention being for these to appear as a subsection of the Arms & Armour Press catalogue. However, coincidentally, it was whilst these discussions were in progress with my then colleagues and a number of outside advisers, that I took the unrelated decision to sell Arms & Armour Press. As the negotiations were in progress it was not only agreed that the short-run publications were not part of the plans of the new owners but also, it being a condition of 'non competition' in the contract for the sale of Arms & Armour Press, that I would be restricted for a period of time from issuing new military books. Hence the new owners, Link House Books Limited, were happy for me to undertake this low intensity publishing activity.

The name Greenhill was chosen because it was sufficiently general to cover a wide range of subjects, the inspiration being the locally well-known 'Greenhill' site in Hampstead High Street upon which I looked out for many years from my desk in the Arms & Armour Press office. The tree logo was developed from a wood engraving by Thomas Bewick (1753-1828). The initial publishing programme ranged from the *Vintage Aviation Library* to *Vintage Crime Classics* (edited by me) and *Vintage Science Fiction and Fantasy* (edited by Brian Stableford).

I stayed with Arms & Armour Press for two years after the

sale. The business was gradually integrated into that of Link House Books in Poole and it was sad to see members of the team that I had built depart, but the Greenhill Books list gradually developed during this period. As it did so it became apparent that it was those books on military subjects that were developing most strongly and the (enjoyable) fiction reprints were gradually phased out. We still, however, receive enquiries from time to time for books by Edgar Wallace, for example; there seems to be an audience for them out there somewhere.

The sale of Arms & Armour Press, coinciding with the publication of the first Greenhill books, took place in October 1984 and the offices in Hampstead were maintained for a further two years. In October 1986, Link House Books closed the Hampstead office and shortly thereafter sold their group of seven book publishing houses to Cassell (and Cassell itself was subsequently taken over by Orion which was taken over by a French publishing conglomerate).

My link with Arms & Armour Press was then severed, although I had hoped that there might have been some sort of continuing role, and I was never contacted again (in the prover-bial expression, even to ask the time of day). At that time I was moving home and, due to the vagaries of the house market, was caught in the trap of having a new house but not yet selling the old. This enabled my office contents of books, files, furniture and so forth to be moved into the garage of the old, where it was packed solid (to be out of immediate sight as potential purchasers were shown around) and a couple of desks to be set up on the bare boards of an empty, echoing lounge. Greenhill's modest publishing was able to continue and, at the end of June 1987, was moved into Park House, Russell Gardens, London NW11. Lynda Jones, my long-standing secretary (who had joined me in 1973) moved with me, and still works with me, and David Gibbons (who had joined me in 1969) plus Tony Evans (who joined in 1973) set up a freelance design team which continues to work to this day on our new books.

The first Greenhill books were reissues of two classics about World War I aviation: *Immelmann: The Eagle of Lille* and *Rovers of the Night Sky*. These were released on 25th October 1984, with simple blue covers. The following February, two books in the *Vintage Crime Classics* appeared, and both series continued to be published for several years. Twenty-four volumes were produced in the *Vintage Aviation Library* (two, *The Red Air Fighter* and *Flying Fury*, have recently been reprinted) and twelve in the *Vintage Crime Classics*. Six volumes appeared in the *Vintage Science Fiction and Fantasy Classics*.

It was as the two 'Vintage' series appeared that I received a letter from Random House in New York saying that we should not use that word. I protested, pointing out that the books were turn-of-the-century classics and the word fitted them perfectly, and that they could not take the word out of the English language. They disagreed. I pointed out that people talked, wrote and published about vintage champagne and wine, or cars, or many other things. Random House said that they had trade-marked the word in respect of its use for publishing, and we should prepare for litigation. I quoted Marx v Warner Brothers: when the Marx Brothers announced that they were going to make a film called *A Night in Casablanca*, Warner Brothers undertook litigation claiming that this could be confused with their Humphrey Bogart film *Casablanca*. Argument ensued, and when Warner Brothers' lawyers asked for the script of the Marx Brothers film they received so many confusing and contradictory plots they were left totally bemused. But then Marx Brothers counter-sued Warner Brothers, saying that their act had appeared first on the vaudeville stage, and hence they had a prior claim over the use of the word 'Brothers', and Warner Brothers should cease their usage of the word. The claim and counter-claim disappeared.

I had a meeting in New York, and Random House entirely agreed that my publishing was of no danger to them, they expressed friendship, but said that they would certainly proceed with legal action, and of course had in-house attorneys for such. They didn't regard it as anything personal but they had to defend the name 'vintage' in case some bigger fish than I came along. Hence shortly thereafter the word 'vintage' disappeared from series titles of the books, to be replaced by Greenhill.

Other fiction published by Greenhill included books by Arnold Bennett, Arthur Conan Doyle, Joseph Conrad, John Galsworthy, Ellery Queen and Israel Zangwill.

The first non-aviation, military book Greenhill published was *The Journal of the Waterloo Campaign* by General Cavalié Mercer, which appeared in August 1985, the first book also in the *Napoleonic Library*, in which thirty-five titles have been published.

In the early years of Greenhill all the publications were reprints or reissues, although sometimes one had to question whether a book created from material that had never been presented in a stand-alone book format was or was not a reprint (such as *The Campaign of Waterloo* by Sir John Fortescue, or *Arms and Equipment of the British Army* with additional material by John Walter, or the English-language presentation of *The Exercise of Armes* by Jacob de Gheyn). One pressure was that many bookshops or public libraries defined 'reprint' as something which had appeared in any format, at any time, and therefore they would not stock it, and this kept the print-runs low and restricted Greenhill's capabilities. I always asked whether, if Shakespeare had been out of print and restored to availability, they would say that they would not stock it, but that argument never got me anywhere.

Through the latter half of the 1980s many fine books were made available, including:

Wellington's Army, 1809–1814 by Sir Charles Oman
The Exercise of Armes by Jacob de Gheyn
Napoleonic Military History: A Bibliography edited by
    Donald D. Horward (reprinted from a US-published
    book)
Dictionary of Military Terms compiled by the US Joint
    Chiefs of Staff
Ships of the Royal Navy by J. J. Colledge (revised edition)
A History of the Art of War in the 16th Century by
    Sir Charles Oman
Lost Victories by Field Marshal Erich von Manstein
The Military Maxims of Napoleon with a new commentary
    by David Chandler
*Commando Men: The Story of a Royal Marine Commando
    in World War II* by Bryan Samain
In Zululand with the British Throughout the War of 1879
    (Greenhill's first of a number of books about the
    Anglo-Zulu War, published in July 1988)
The Memoirs of Field-Marshal Kesselring

And then in October 1988 came a significant event: the publication of Greenhill's first wholly and completely original book requiring new setting, *The Royal Navy in World War II: A Bibliographic Guide* by D. G. Law. This book sets what I believe are the ideal standards for any quality bibliography, in terms of access, subject classification and, in particular, comments about each book which put it into perspective. I have a collection of bibliographies on military history, and I continue to use this fine reference book today.

The strong programme of reissues, reprints and revised editions still continued, however, with books such as:

Storm from the Sea by Peter Young
The Seafire: The Spitfire that Went to Sea by David Brown
(revised edition)
Long Range Desert Group by W. B. Kennedy Shaw, with a
new Introduction by David Lloyd Owen
War Books: An Annotated Bibliography by Cyril Falls,
updated by R. J. Wyatt
Bomber Offensive by Sir Arthur Harris, with a new
Introduction by Denis Richards
Fuehrer Conferences on Naval Affairs with a new
Introduction by Jak Mallman Showell
Doenitz: Memoirs – Ten Years and Twenty Days with new
material by Jürgen Rohwer

It was at this time that we had an all-time best excuse from a printer when we were seeking confirmation of a schedule for the production of a book. We called to check on progress, to be told 'Sorry, the printing press has been stolen.' Yes, there had been a break-in by an obviously knowledgeable and experienced team, and a new Heidelberg printing press had been uplifted and removed. To add insult to injury, it was removed in one of the printer's own trucks. The police were said to have advised that such thefts on a 'to order' basis were not unknown, and the equipment was probably over on the Continent in a matter of hours. The printer did however organise things so that the book still just met its production schedule.

Greenhill leapt properly on to the new book publishing stage with a significant and substantial book in May 1990: *Brave Men's Blood: The Epic of the Zulu War, 1879* by Ian Knight. This is a large-format book, with a strong text and 270 illustrations, and eventually was reprinted as a large-format trade paperback. It has certainly been one of Greenhill's best-selling titles.

Then in April 1991 came a blockbuster: *Soviet Wings: Modern Soviet Military Aircraft* by Alexander Dzhus. *Soviet Wings* was a large-format book with brilliant photographs. It grew out of a conversation held on a Russian publisher's stand at the Frankfurt Book Fair in October 1989, and led to the somewhat difficult dinner party I described in chapter seven. The start of it all was when the publisher showed me a maquette of a book about the history of Soviet aviation, which had photographs over the last century and through World War II. There was one very grainy photograph of a modern plane. I had already put the book to one side, saying that I did not see an audience for it, when something made me ask if the grainy photograph was in colour. 'Da' was the answer. I was astonished; the photograph was of a Tu-160 Blackjack in flight above the clouds. Those were the days of Gorbachev, when there was a new atmosphere even though the Soviet Union was still a major world power and a major military threat, and after a little hesitation I asked 'Do you have other such photographs?' Again the answer was 'Da'. I put forward the idea of undertaking a wholly new book, in full colour, on modern Soviet aircraft, rather than their general, overall project. I was not ejected from the stand, I was not given the standard answer used so many times over the years in negotiating with the Soviets, that it was 'not expedient'. Instead they asked how many such pictures I would like to have! Desperately trying not to show undue enthusiasm, I asked for 150. Nobody fell over at this suggestion, and indeed they started asking as to what sort of contract we would give them.

Over the next months I received a series of slide boxes with transparencies, and I showed these to one or two knowledgeable friends. They were excited. They were, in fact, electrified. Things were being sent to us that had never been seen in the West before. Technical details previously unknown were now being revealed. A little team of people from Whitehall came up to our Golders Green offices a number of times in order to inspect the pictures. When I was in Washington, word via one of my contacts reached the CIA, and a team came into my hotel on a Sunday afternoon to inspect the photographs (and pose some pretty pointed questions as to why these pictures were coming to me). One friend in Washington said that they had never seen a photograph of a Su-27 Flanker taking off from an aircraft carrier, and I passed this and a shopping list of other suggested requirements through to Moscow. Materials came to us during the course of the year (including a whole sequence of photographs showing the Flanker taking off and landing from the aircraft carrier *Tiblisi)* and when I returned to Washington my contacts were bug-eyed and stunned that I was producing such images. Were they not now going to be freely available I could have sold them for a lot of money.

A contract was signed, and for the Frankfurt Book Fair 1990 we had a dummy, sample pages, and forecast costs. We signed up a whole team of foreign-language publishers who wanted to join the print-run for what was then sensational material. Those were the days when it also looked as though the hard-liners would take over again in the Soviet Union, and none of us knew when the source that had enabled such material to come to us might be cut off. We safely received sufficient material to make a stunning book, and then flew like bats out of hell to fulfil the contractual arrangements which saw the book appear in several English-language editions (including Canadian), and translations into Japanese, German, Italian, French and Slovak, all in one 50,000 copy print-run.

As *Soviet Wings* was published the Soviet Union went into collapse, and there was no longer the frisson of excitement in being able to see photographs of their aircraft. Yes, the book was stunning and beautiful, revealing sensational new things, but interest in Cold War military equipment also collapsed as the Cold War came to an end. We sold the first copies of the book extremely quickly, and then the sale stopped almost overnight. When the Soviet negotiating team sat down with us at the 1991 Fair and we all congratulated ourselves on a very successful project, and a considerable sum of money having been paid in royalties, they asked 'What would you like next, Mr Leventhal? We would be able now to produce a project on nuclear submarines.' I had to respond that peace was not good for military publishing. Fortunately, by that time we had completed all of our supply contracts, and *Soviet Wings* was probably the most profitable single project ever undertaken by Greenhill books in the shortest possible time.

1991 was good for Greenhill Books due to the Iraqi invasion of Kuwait. We were working at that time with Colonel Trevor Dupuy of Washington, who produced a little booklet entitled *If War Comes.* We ended up air-freighting quantities of the book, and sold several thousand. Immediately after the war a large format book, *Desert Storm: The Gulf War in Colour,* was produced on a co-edition basis with an Italian publisher, and we sold a large number in a very short period. In August 1991 we produced on a rush basis a fine multi-author study entitled *Military Lessons of the Gulf War,* edited by the late Bruce Watson, which was a Main Choice for the military book clubs on both sides of the Atlantic, sold successfully and was translated into several languages (including Chinese).

By the early 1990s Greenhill had taken significant steps towards creating the infrastructure to enable the publishing house to undertake a programme of wholly new books. Rather like the evolution from a monkey to mankind, Greenhill had progressed from:

¶ a reprint with simple cover
¶ to a reprint with simple cover and new introduction
¶ to a reprint with designed cover
¶ to a reprint with designed cover and new material
¶ to a reissue of hitherto inaccessible source works
¶ to a reissue of hitherto inaccessible source works, with new introduction
¶ to a reissue of hitherto inaccessible source works with new introduction and illustrations
¶ to reprints and reissues with fully designed covers of a trade nature
¶ to printing first British editions of new books from America for trade publication
¶ to wholly new books of a specialist nature
¶ to wholly new books of a general specialist nature.

A significant step in the growth and development of the new Greenhill publishing house occurred when there were sufficient books and continuity for Presidio of California to undertake distribution of the Greenhill list in the USA, and Greenhill to distribute Presidio internationally. This commenced in 1989, and Greenhill distributes Presidio's books to this day. However, when Presidio changed their warehousing and sales representation in 1993, Greenhill transferred distribution to Stackpole Books.

The current vigorous and solid Greenhill publishing programme of new books is effectively only a dozen years old (or, rather, young). Authors with whom Greenhill has had the privilege of working in recent years include:

Paul Britten Austin	Chaim Herzog	Kenneth Macksey
David Chandler	Peter Hofschröer	Dr Alfred Price
Christopher Duffy	Ian V. Hogg	Jürgen Rohwer
Colonel John Elting	David C. Isby	Digby Smith
Jeffrey Ethell	Ian Knight	Mike Spick
Mordechai Gichon	John Langellier	Peter Tsouras
John H. Gill	Cecil Lewis	Andrew Uffindell
Paddy Griffith	James Lucas	Bruce Watson

18

AUTHORS

ONE OF THE GREAT PLEASURES OF PUBLISHING is working with authors. I have been quoted as saying that working with books that are in the public domain is a treat for, obviously, if the author is unfortunately long since deceased, he cannot but be happy with the new book jacket, the presentation of the book, the advertising and reviews and all we are doing to present his work to a new generation. Although working on the books of long-deceased authors may be quieter, it is certainly not as stimulating as working with an author who can help create a quality book from a thorough knowledge of a specific subject; one misses the creative interplay and stimulation that one experiences when working with a wholly new book by a living author.

I have had the pleasure of working with many fine authors, stimulating and very alive, and it is difficult to choose who to write about.

Perhaps one should start at the top, with the President of a country. In 1982 I published *The Arab-Israeli Wars* by Chaim Herzog. At that time Chaim Herzog (known to his friends as Vivian) was the Israeli Ambassador to the United Nations. I had commissioned him to write a book about the Arab–Israeli wars. Each time I was in New York I would meet him at the Israeli Legation and we discussed the work in progress on the book. On one visit, after a long review of material and discussion about restructuring the book (I had had to find a way to tell him that, as he was a natural raconteur, he should dictate the key sections rather than write them, for when writing he reverted in style to that necessary in his professional career as a lawyer), Vivian had to depart for the United Nations. We had not quite finished our conversation and Vivian said, 'Come with me, we can finish the conversation in the car.' Escorted by outriders, the ambassadorial limousine made the journey to the United Nations building and as it swept up alongside, so did we finish the conversation. When we drew up, Vivian said, 'Come in with us, Lionel. You can join the Israeli delegation in the Security Council and listen to us being denounced and my response. I'm going to tell them they are a bunch of liars.' I declined, and explained that I was running late for another meeting. Vivian leapt from the car, and instructed the driver to deliver me to my next rendezvous. He dashed off and the limousine took me across New York to my meeting. Alas, when I arrived I discovered that the meeting that I was rushing for had been cancelled, and after all I had a spare couple of hours.

The sale of *The Arab-Israeli Wars* was however severely affected because at the time of our launch the Argentinians had invaded the Falklands, and the British armed forces were on the way to the South Atlantic. During this period all news broadcasts were totally dominated by that news, and although Vivian had come to London for the launch, everyone was preoccupied with the Falklands Conflict.

About eighteen months later my wife and I, with our children, made a holiday visit to Israel. By this time Herzog had become President and as a courtesy I let him know that I would be on holiday, but assuming that he had a full and busy schedule did not expect to hear from him.

One day the family were out on tour and as we came back to the hotel the hotel management had someone standing outside watching for our return. As soon as we drove up, the manager was informed and came rushing over. 'The President's private secretary has called for confirmation for the lunch on Sunday.' And anxiously asked 'Do we need to make arrangements?'

We returned the call to Herzog's office and, yes, we were invited to his family home in Herzliya for lunch the following

Sunday. Our hotel manager relaxed, for he had already started considering security and hospitality arrangements should the President be visiting us. We enjoyed our visit to the home of Aura and Vivian. We remember with amusement he advised our daughter, Louise, that learning Latin served no useful purpose. She was delighted to have reason promptly to abandon it in school. Later on in our break we visited him in the presidential palace in Jerusalem (actually on Christmas Day), and among the subjects discussed were possible future publications and Vivian's memoirs, which I said should be published by a major general publishing trade house (and they appeared as *Living History* from Weidenfeld & Nicolson).

Vivian and I remained in contact and a couple of years ago whilst I was researching books on military aspects of the ancient world, I noticed that *Battles of the Bible*, which he had written with Mordechai Gichon, was out of print. This had been published in 1978 by Weidenfeld. 'How about reissuing it?' I asked. He was happy with this suggestion, and so was Professor Gichon, who did a great deal of work for the new edition which was published in 1997.

The new edition of *Battles of the Bible* was published by Greenhill coincidentally at the same time. Vivian came to London to launch his autobiography and, again, our publication of a book by him was overshadowed for, of course, the media paid considerable attention to the publication of his remarkable memoirs. I attended one lecture presentation he gave, and helped the sale of *Living History* but managed to sneak in the name of *Battles of the Bible*. Herzog was always a warm friendly man, like a favourite uncle. He never struck me as a man of remarkable intellect, rather he had an inner gyroscope, with stability and vision, and throughout the tumultuous period of the founding of the State of Israel, the wars and fierce Middle East politics, he kept the most even, straight and moral course.

He was a man of remarkable stature, and it was his simple morality and clarity of vision that was outstanding.

On this last visit to London, his schedule was so full that there was no time for my wife and me to be able to entertain him, to reciprocate the hospitality that he had shown us in Israel. We spoke however on the telephone, and he wanted to arrange the publication of a new edition of his book *The War of Atonement*, a classic about the 1973 Yom Kippur war. I confess, somewhat tongue in cheek, that I made the condition of republication that he should have dinner with us the next time that he and his wife were in London. However, very sadly, Vivian died a couple of weeks later. The new edition of *The War of Atonement*, with an introduction by his son, appeared in 1998.

One thing that I have endeavoured to do over the years is to have the authors of the book that I have published sign copies to me. I have an extensive collection in my study, going back over many years. Herzog's *Battles of the Bible* was signed for me by him just a few weeks before his death, and movingly reads: 'In friendship'.

All authors have different personalities, naturally, and I always work closely with them, often in partnership, to produce the best possible books. Quite a number of authors have had their first books published by me at Arms & Armour Press or Greenhill, and many have continued with a long authorship career.

19

WORKING WITH
DEAD AUTHORS

A MAJOR PROBLEM WITH REISSUING A BOOK that has been out of print can be locating the copyright holder. If the book is still in copyright, then a licence to publish is needed and in preference one should be in touch with the residual legatee of the author's estate. I have always preferred this to going to the original publisher. If you do so, the original publisher may well have no knowledge at all about the rights if the book was published many years ago or prior to a succession of takeovers, or may take all the licence fee. He may be out of touch with the residual legatee and not interested to do the research, and hence will retain monies that come in, and although this would not be my problem I think it unfair. Perhaps even in being reminded about a long-out-of-print book he will be precipitated into undertaking a reprint himself, or just be avaricious.

Hence over the years we have had to undertake research to locate estates, and this can be something of an exercise in detection.

In Britain the term of copyright used to be for the author's life plus fifty years, so if the author died in 1950 the copyright in his work lasted until the end of the year 2000. This period recently changed to become the author's life plus seventy years, thus the work of the author who died in 1950 will be in copyright until the end of 2020. Hence as at the year 2001 an author would have to have died prior to 1930 for his work to be in the public domain, and for all others you would need a copyright licence.

The first problem occurs because there is no registration system for copyright in Britain. The second is that there is no system for locating the date of somebody's death, and you need that and the place in order to locate the will and probate that would enable you to locate to whom the estate, or copyright, was passed. But even then, if the will is located, the location of the copyright holder might still be something of a puzzle, for people move over the years and to trace a copyright from one estate to another raises wholly different problems and questions.

The change of the terms in copyright from fifty to seventy years has caused us recently to track an estate for an author whom we had previously published when his work was in the public domain. This is Sir John Fortescue, author of the monumental and magnificent *A History of the British Army.* In 1989 we published *The Campaign of Waterloo* by him in our Napoleonic Library. This is a volume presenting an excerpt from the monumental *A History of the British Army*, published on a 'stand-alone' basis for the first time ever. This account of a key British campaign and battle was probably not accessible to many with a special interest in the area, possibly not even thought about because it was part of a significantly larger work.

More recently we decided to publish another excerpt from the British Army history, about the American Revolution, as a separate book for the first time. However, although Sir John Fortescue died in 1933 and his book consequently went into the public domain in 1984, it had come back into copyright with the extension to seventy years, and copyright now extends to 2004.

As Sir John was a significant historian it was relatively simple to obtain the date and place of his death, and send for his will and probate. It was shown that he left his literary work to his wife, Lady Winifred Fortescue. Again because she was fairly well known in her day, and also an author, it was relatively simple to obtain the date and place of her death and her will and probate. Lady Winifred died in 1951 and left Sir John's copyrights to his great nephew, saying:

'in so far as such books articles or other literary works have been written by my late Husband then to his great nephew

Timothy Carew of Beckhams Manaton Devonshire in the certainty that out of his love and respect for his Godfather he will arrange with the various publishers for necessary reprints and editions and will find someone competent to correct the proofs as carefully as his Godfather would have wished.'

We knew the name of Tim Carew as an author, but he was referred to bibliographically with the initials J. M. and hence, as we couldn't see an informal name or nickname being used in a legal document, we didn't think that it could be the same person. But how to find 'Beckhams Manaton'? The Devonshire Records Office soon put us right: Beckhams was a house in the village of Manaton. Directory Enquiries had no telephone number for Timothy Carew, and hence we telephoned the nearest public library to check the voters' register. They advised the name of the family who were living there, and we wrote to them and followed this up with a telephone call. They had lived in the house for thirty or more years, and knew nothing about Mr Timothy Carew. They however knew someone in the village who had lived there for a much longer time and said they would have a word with him. So I called back a few days later to be advised that Mr Timothy Carew had moved in the early 1950s to somewhere in the Thames Valley. The person thought the place he had moved to was Blewbury.

We had no address to go on, but again tried Directory Enquiries who advised that there was an ex-directory number for a Carew in Blewbury, and also a number of other Carews in the area. They would not, however, provide the address of the house in Blewbury, and without the address we could not call the local library to see if they could check the voters' register to see if it was Mr Timothy who lived there, or if the current house-holder knew anything about him.

Doing some lateral thinking, and hoping that in fact the Timothy Carew in the will might be the author of several books such as *The Fall of Hong Kong*, we wrote letters to the three or four publishers who had published his books, but had no success in locating an address for him. Continuing with lateral thought, we contacted Lieutenant Colonel R. J. Wyatt, a long-standing friend, with exceptional knowledge of the history of the British Army, and a fine collection of books. Did he by chance know of Timothy Carew, because he lived also in the Thames Valley? Yes, he advised; he remembered Carew's collection of books being sold some years earlier through a second-hand book dealer. He promised to make enquiries and when we spoke to him a few days later he was able to advise a telephone number of a house where the son of Timothy Carew lived, in the Bracknell area of close-by Blewbury. We telephoned, and were directed to the family solicitors.

This then led to solving the question whether the Timothy Carew in Lady Winifred Fortescue's will was one and the same as the Timothy Carew the author, whose initials were J. M. He had died in 1980 and had left his estate to his wife, who had died in 1993 and left her estate to their daughter. Yes, there was a straight line and the solicitor was able to act on her behalf, and a licence arrangement was made through their help with the granddaughter of the great nephew of the author granting permission to us for the rest of the period of copyright, until 2004, for the recent publication of *The War of Independence* by Sir John Fortescue.

A much longer and more difficult case was tracing Captain C. Shore, author of *With British Snipers to the Reich*. Although by a Briton and about British fighting in World War II, Shore's book was only published in the United States, in 1948. When visiting Washington DC I made a check at the Library of Congress and viewed the original copyright application form, which showed that the book was registered for copyright in January 1949 and the address was given as 'Hazel Grove, Stockport'. However, that created a problem, for Hazel Grove is an area, not a residential address. The Library of Congress information indicated that Shore had been born in 1908 and hence he would at the time of our search have been either nearly ninety years old, or more likely long since deceased.

The first thing I did when I was back in England was to check the telephone directory for the area, and there was no C. Shore in Hazel Grove. There were twenty-four Shores living in the area and we telephoned all of them, but none had heard of C. Shore who was living there in the 1948/1949 period.

In the book there are mentions of several regiments with which Shore served, for as a member of Britain's special forces in World War II he moved around from regiment to regiment according to need. We were able to establish that he was a flying officer, which was fairly unusual for special forces, but from this we checked with the RAF Regiment Comrades Association, the RAF Regimental Museum, the Royal Air Force Museum in Hendon, and had a notice published in RAF News, all without result. At one stage it was believed that he was a member of the Royal Artillery Regiment, and so we checked with the Royal Artillery Institution. There was reference in the book to the Lovat Scouts, but the Lovat Scouts Association and the Lovat Scouts Regimental Museum could not help us. Neither could the School of Infantry. Because he was a rifleman we tried also the National Rifle Association, which he mentions in the book, but their records did not help us.

We went back to the Stockport Public Library and asked them to check a 1949 telephone directory. Bingo! That provided a street address. We had them check the current voters' register for that address, but the family there had only moved in in recent years and obviously would have no information about somebody who had lived there so many years earlier. We checked back every five years or so through the voters' register in case we could establish a straight line, but for whatever reason it seems that people from that address changed relatively frequently. What we did establish was that the initial 'C.'

stood for Clifford, and that his wife's name was Hannah. He was at that address at the time of the publication of the book and a few years afterwards, but then his name dropped from the voters' register and shortly thereafter his wife's name disappeared.

It seems that we had reached a dead end, with no way to trace Clifford Shore or his descendants through military channels, or through his address.

As one last resort, as we had not been able to find anyone with a connection to Shore's address we moved sideways, and checked the occupants of the adjacent houses, on both sides, all the way back to 1949. We found that one side had had the same occupant since that time, and somewhat in desperation we wrote to that lady, told her what we were trying to do, and said that we would telephone in a few days' time (a telephone number again being located by means of checking with the local library).

We telephoned, and incredibly we found that she was living in what had been Shore's house. We were told that the street had been renumbered, and hence this was the building that the Shores had lived in since Clifford Shore had died and Hannah also. Even more incredible, she was in touch with their daughter who was going to visit her so that they could go for church choir practice in about half an hour's time.

It was rather like a television programme where people find long lost relatives and tell them that they are going to inherit some money, but I was happy to telephone, speak to the married daughter and establish the link. The daughter had been ten years old when her father died but she was able to provide the documentation that confirmed the situation, and enabled us to undertake a publishing agreement with her and republish the book.

This was probably the longest and most complicated search we have undertaken, and we are not sure if there is a moral from the fact that the search became more interesting than the resulting book, which eventually had to be remaindered.

20

IN MEMORIAM

WITH THE PASSAGE OF TIME one is conscious that a number of good people with whom one has worked, sometimes very closely, are no longer around. I think that this reflects one's own age; when I started in publishing everyone I worked with was older than myself. As one progresses, things even up a little, although there are always extremes. Now there are only a small, but important, number of authors older, and most are contemporary and a good number much younger.

I noticed fifteen or so years ago that from time to time, possibly every year or two, people whom I respected and enjoyed working with passed away. This saddened me, but because I had so many good memories of them I didn't want to forget them. Hence to celebrate and remember such friends I have kept a list at the back of my diary to which I unfortunately have to add names periodically, but when I do I read over those who have gone before and have good memories of enjoyable relationships.

The oldest author, in years but not in mind, was Cecil Lewis who died in his ninety-ninth year. He was a World War I aviator who flew over the Somme battlefield and then had a long and remarkable life, with careers and adventures in many very different areas. I was first in touch with Cecil in 1990 when he was ninety-two years old. Word had reached me that he was working on a companion volume to his classic *Sagittarius Rising*, to be entitled *Sagittarius Surviving* and dealing with World War II. I wrote to him in Corfu, where he and his wife Fanny had their home, to ask if it was something we might consider publishing. By the time my letter reached him he had already offered it to another publisher. One thing that characterised Cecil to the end was his sharp brain, and in his response he said:

'You know what the book trade is at present. All serious authors are against these huge conglomerates who treat authors disgracefully and are only interested in shameful moneygrubbing. I take it your firm has no part in one? I am not playing off one publisher against another: but I am ninety-two and this is probably my last book. It will not be a best-seller, but will probably go on, like SAG, for fifty years. I don't know where to place it, frankly. I am waiting for a sign.'

Leo Cooper accepted *Sagittarius Surviving* with alacrity, but Cecil and I started a correspondence, with long, detailed and chatty letters about publishing and Life (very much with a capital 'L').

About a year later he was to be in London and we arranged to meet, he writing: 'I feel this is all rather like a "blind date" – though, mercifully, with none of the heart throbs that used to precede such thrilling moments in days of long ago! However I promise not to arrive with a bunch of roses and trust you will save yourself the expense of a diamond ring.'

Cecil may have been in his nineties, but he was still over six feet high, if slightly stooped, and still a very handsome gentleman with a twinkle in his eye and a sense of humour.

We corresponded at length, regularly (in fact a sort of author/publisher version of *84 Charing Cross Road*, albeit less literary) and this led a couple of years later to my reprinting the great World War I aviation classic *Sagittarius Rising*. He wrote a new Introduction and came to London for his ninety-fifth birthday, the very successful relaunching of the book and the seventy-fifth birthday celebrations of the Royal Air Force. For the RAF anniversary we had created with the RAF Museum the book *High Flyers* which gathered together newly written stories of the careers of many who had served, such as Michael Bentine, Frederick Forsyth, Hughie Green, Gavin Lyall, Cliff Michelmore,

C. Northcote Parkinson, Kenneth Wolstenholme, etc. etc., there
being, overall, thirty contributors. Each contributor handwrote a
word of greeting which was reproduced in facsimile at the front
of the book. Cecil's was 'Patriarchal Greetings! From one who
lived those early days', but he provided an alternative: 'From
galloping horse to Concorde!'

Coinciding with all of this the *Sunday Telegraph* colour
magazine published a feature about Cecil, sending an interviewer and photographer out to Corfu. The story of his life of
astounding activity included the nugget that he had shared 'his
bed with half a thousand women'. After World War I, he
emerged 'into peace time at the age of twenty-one, with the
looks and appetite of a sensual Greek God, and the aesthetic
instincts of a poet'.

Although his romantic life only formed a part of his story as
told in the feature, apparently as an anecdote mentioned to the
interviewer in a moment of relaxation from talking about his
life, it acquired a larger significance in the article. His wife was
not pleased.

The next time that he was interviewed for the British press he
seemed to distance himself a little, and put his previous
comments about the *joie de vivre* of his youth into perspective,
saying: 'As a young man I was very much over-sexed, and it's a
joy but it doesn't last. It is very trivial, momentary and, in the
end, simply not enough.'

At that time Cecil worked closely with and was a good friend
of many in London's finest literary and media circles, including
George Bernard Shaw. Once, when he was hard up, he asked if he
could sell Shaw's correspondence with him, and was immediately
and enthusiastically requested to sell for as much as he could.

Cecil, with his wife Fanny, and Elizabeth and I, got together
every time when they were in London. We never spoke about his
World War I career, for although his view of the world was
dystopic he also wanted to know about what was happening,

the latest computer system, and what young people were doing. From his viewpoint, World War I and his book *Sagittarius Rising* had taken place a very long time ago, more than the lifetime of an ordinary person.

Cecil remained active until the end, writing a couple of books in his nineties, and poetry. He told me however that he took up writing sonnets, because he did not know how much longer he had left. He also took to telephoning rather than writing, and, sensitive to interrupting a meeting that I was in, was kind enough to ask if I minded. 'Not at all, Cecil,' I said, adding 'but if you write I would be able to eventually sell your letters.' There was a pause, and then his characteristic warm laugh.

I booked him for the publication of a new edition of *Sagittarius Rising* to be published on his 100th birthday, but he died in January 1997, in London, just fifteen months short. He did not die directly due to illness, or old age. He had gone into a hospital in Greece for a routine operation, an ingrowing toenail or something like that, but picked up an infection. The RAF flew him back to a hospital in London, but by that time it was too late to save him.

I knew Cecil Lewis for too short a time.

Another good friend and author whom fortunately I had the pleasure of knowing for many years, and who lived to a good age, but also died too soon, was Colonel John Elting in the United States. John was a kind man, a master of military history. He was courteous, like a Southern gentleman, and his knowledge was probably the most extensive that I have ever experienced. His great knowledge was not just of the detail, but he had perspective and often saw things with a sense of humour.

When we were working on the monumental encyclopaedia compiled by Digby Smith and published as *The Greenhill Napoleonic Wars Data Book*, for our invigilation process we broke the content into periods and shared it amongst fourteen specialist experts. John's range of knowledge was such that he

Many who have this essential book in their collection do not realise how good the text is, and indeed how good John's bibliography is, with extremely apposite but brief critical comments. He tried to keep his visits over to London as brief as possible, for he wanted to be away from his wife for the minimum period. It was in fact Ann who was somewhat unwell, and who never really recovered from an unfortunate fall a year or two earlier. We held a special luncheon for him on the Saturday before each event, and for the Napoleonic Fair he not only gave a presentation at each he attended but also spent the whole day meeting people, talking to people, and being characteristically helpful. For the first visit the journey was truly a 'journey from hell' for his travel agent had given him a strange routing, but then because it was in February it coincided with one of the major snow falls on the Eastern coast of the United States. I think the plan was that he would fly out of New York, but he was diverted to Washington, and then rediverted to Boston, before the international flight. Although I was waiting at the airport, no word about this reached me, and he ended up having to find his own way into central London. But he was still full of vim and vigour for the lunch the next day, and the following day for the Napoleonic Fair. His travel adventures sounded like something from the John Candy film *Planes, Trains and Automobiles*, where everything that could possibly go wrong did.

On his second visit for the Napoleonic Fair he once again had a very full day, and afterwards I drove him and his friends Mr and Mrs Bill Hurlbutt back to his hotel. Bill Hurlbutt told me later that he and his wife, too, had had a full day and were ready for a very leisurely lazy evening, but John kept them entertained, they had a most enjoyable dinner, and it proved to be a fairly late night. How John kept going like that was wonderful, and Bill thought he knew that this would be his last hurrah.

He had by that time been told by his doctor that he was far from well, and shortly thereafter he was told he did not have a great deal of time left. He wrote several warm and gracious letters which, read with the benefit of hindsight, were effectively saying farewell. However a short while later I was going to be in New York and I made arrangements to visit with him, working things out so that I could drive up to his home. I called from my hotel to confirm the arrangements to meet him, had a little conversation, and then went out on business. When I returned to my hotel I heard the sad news that he had died, peacefully at his desk, just two hours after our conversation.

John's death was a shock. I knew that he was very ill, but he was so cogent, so brain alert, that it was as though a vital person half of his age had passed away in an untimely fashion. John left too few of his own books, but his memory will stay alive through those that he fostered and encouraged, and to those whom he gave freely of his knowledge.

I maintained my plan to visit the Elting home, just two days after he passed away, and spent time with Ann. Ann and John would have celebrated their sixty-fifth wedding anniversary just a few months later. Ann said that I should go into his study and take a book as a memento. I had a look at the books, with which I was familiar from previous visits, but it was noteworthy that his collection was a working one rather than of historic and collectable volumes. Indeed, a number of his books were those that I had published. However he also had some toy soldiers, and with Ann's kind permission I took a figure of Napoleon on a grey horse, which is in front of me as I write this memoir.

John's last letter to me was dated a few days before I was due to go over to the United States to see him. It started: 'Unfortunately, it looks as though this is serious. Shall have to check myself back into hospital tomorrow – state of utter exhaustion, plus, plus, plus. No "Get Well" cards please!'

John was in his ninetieth year when he died.

A most untimely death was that of Jeffrey L. Ethell, the American aviation book author. Again I had known Jeff, and his wife

Bettie, since the late 1970s or early 1980s (the first book of his I published appeared in 1983). Jeff was killed in a tragic flying accident, flying a P-38 Lightning in a rehearsal for a Warbirds show in Oregon. The aircraft had been painted in the colours of his father's wartime aeroplane, and as the plane came in to land with both Jeff's wife and father watching, it passed behind a hangar, and never came into view again on the other side.

Since the time when he had been a little boy, and obviously under his father's influence, Jeff had been interested in aviation. As a historian and researcher he wrote many books and built an immensely valuable collection of photographs. He had the practicality of someone who has a commanding knowledge of the subject area.

As part of collecting materials he went about the various veterans' associations, or communicated via their newsletters, to collect memoirs and especially photographs. He built a vast archive of both black-and-white photographs and colour images. The perceived wisdom at that time was that colour images of the war did not exist. Jeff proved otherwise. What Jeff demonstrated was that many of the serving airmen in World War II had taken cameras with them, with the latest Kodak film. At that time Kodak film could only be developed in the United States, and film was either sent back home and sent for developing, or awaited the return of the person who took the photo. Also such was the chemical processing in Kodak that the film was stable and did not degrade and is still as good today as it was when it was originally taken. However with people returning from war and getting on with their lives, the developed film slides were usually put away. It was only when Jeff started asking for such images that he received a steady flow, and built a collection of over 20,000. Although his interest was in the aircraft, young men coming to war photograph all sorts of attractive things. There are lots of photographs of downtown London in World War II, with Eros in Piccadilly boarded up and a famous club opposite. And lots of young ladies. And village greens and pubs. And lots of young ladies.

Based on his collection of photographs Jeff produced quite a number of valuable books, including *G.I. Victory* (with David C. Isby) which I published.

Jeff and his family were devout, committed Christians, and Jeff was ordained as a minister of the Baptist church. There is no suggestion here of being fundamentalist; he and Bettie, and the whole family, were open, kind and gentle people. Whenever I was in Washington DC I would endeavour to visit with them at their home in Front Royal, Virginia, or if I could not then he and Bettie, and sometimes the children, came to dinner in Washington. In his home we would sit at the wooden table in their kitchen to eat, and he would say grace and I would add the Hebrew blessing over bread. We discussed comparative religion, and I think that he knew more than me. One discussion about the transition from sacrifice to no sacrifice for sin, I had to refer back to my Rabbi, Rabbi Alan Plancey of the Elstree and Borehamwood Syna-gogue, for a ruling. Another time when I had to consult my Rabbi was following a query raised by Harris Colt of New York's Mili-tary Bookman bookshop. He had found a quotation attributable to 'Ben Bag Bag', which he found difficult to take seriously. I had never heard of Ben Bag Bag, but Rabbi Plancey had no problem in advising that he was a first-century sage.

One measure of my respect for Jeff was when, quite some years ago, he had some sort of financial problem and called to ask what book or books he could prepare, preferably quickly, in order to raise some money. My question to him was 'How much do you need?', and I sent a cheque to him that night, for I knew that we could work out a project, preferred not to do so on an emergency basis, and could trust him to honour any arrange-ment at a future date.

A week before Jeff's tragic and untimely death his first grand-child was born.

In Memoriam

My list full of warm memories of authors whom I have worked with and have lost over the last fifteen years is:

26.5.87	Peter Dickens	17.4.97	Chaim Herzog
10.9.89	Bil Hughes	6.6.97	Jeff Ethell
6.5.93	Bruce Watson	20.7.98	A. V. B. Norman
23.12.93	Edward C. Ezell	24.11.99	Howard L. Blackmore
18.8.94	Jac Weller	25.5.00	John Elting
27.1.97	Cecil Lewis	11.8.01	David Brown
6.2.97	W. A. Thorburn	10.2.02	John Erickson

21

PRODUCING BOOKS

DURING MY CAREER there have been more changes in the manu-facturing processes of books than occurred in the previous 500 years. Early in my job with Herbert Jenkins I spent a week at a printers in Beccles, Suffolk, and saw many of the then standard printing processes. These included setting books in metal, on the noisy Monotype or Linotype machines, and handsetting special type sizes, making copper blocks of illustrations and printing from the metal itself. It is in this area that there has been the greatest revolution, and today text is produced directly from the author's disk. Material can be transmitted from computer to computer, and from disk to film and thence to printing plate – and even from disk directly to plate. Illustra-tions which used to be printed from copper blocks are now scanned, digitised and contained on a disk prior to transfer to film. Yesteryear an enormous weight of metal was involved in the production of the books; today it is just a couple of computer disks, some film and a thin metal printing plate.

In the same way that I suggest that anyone seeking to enter book publishing spends time first in a bookshop, so anyone on the editorial side of things should spend time seeing how books are produced. The lessons learned from my week in Beccles all those years ago stayed with me for many, many years. One thing, however, I have yet to achieve. I took with me to Beccles *War and Peace* by Tolstoy to read during the long evenings. I went out every evening after supper into the churchyard, with the book. But such was the calm and peace of the beautiful countryside that I never got into it, and have yet to do so.

In olden days, when I started, if when you were at a printer's and authorising the print run the colours were not to your satisfaction, there were all sorts of black arts that the printer could get up to to make colours lighter or darker, such as shaving the underneath of the wood of a printing block, or even packing paper under it. With offset the black art has gone, although there is much trickery that can be undertaken in the camera room and on the computer. When working on *Butterflies of the World* I went to Holland to authorise the printing and found that the printers there still skilfully married letterpress techniques with offset lithography to massage and get colours right. We worked into the night to perfect colour balances on the printing presses, and it was nearly midnight before we got everything right and went out for something to eat and drink. Somewhat spaced out, during the course of the relaxed conversation I queried to the technical team what techniques we would utilise so as to get the colours right in advance for the next big project. We were working, I said, with the International Institute of Trichology on a book that illustrated human hair. There were to be 27,000 examples that would be illustrated life size, from dark and coarse to fair and light. The Dutch technicians were serious and reviewed possibilities for use of colour backgrounds, extraordinarily fine screens, and so forth, before their British agent who was present realised that this was an example of 'pulling the leg', which then had to be explained.

One fascinating project occurred not with a new book but with reprinting an old one, in the late 1970s. The book was *The Anatomy of Glory*. Originally published in London in the early 1960s by Lund Humphries, on behalf of Brown University Press of Rhode Island, the book had been long out of print. The rights had reverted, and I had undertaken negotiation directly with Brown University Press for a reprint. However, crucial to undertaking the book was the availability of the original colour plates. Blocks of these had been made by a fine art reproduction house in Vienna, and printed by Percy Lund Humphries in Bradford. However as soon as the printing work had been finished, the copper blocks had been sent to Denmark. There was a plan to use them at that time, but nothing came of it. We contacted the Danish printer and he confirmed that he still had the blocks, and indeed had never used them. On this assurance, we proceeded at Arms & Armour Press with the announcement of our edition, and there was an immediate and enthusiastic response. We then, however, had to start the production process, and this is where we ran into a problem.

The blocks were shipped from Denmark to the Norfolk printing plant. The Danish printer was correct in advising that he had never used them; he had never even unwrapped them from their fifteen-year-old storage papers. The printer started to try and do so, but found that the original protective grease had congealed with the wrappings, then dried over the years into a hard lacquered shell. The printer could not open the packed individual blocks! The printer was scared of taking a knife to the wrappings, because if the knife went through and scratched the surface of the copper block that would irreparably damage it. Everyone stood around and gave the matter thought, and the printer had a brain wave. A steam bath! They created a steam bath and individually steamed each copper block, mounted on its wooden support, to loosen the papers, which could then be eased off. So we had access to the blocks, and we gave the printing order.

Then the printer phoned with another problem. It was discovered that in the fifteen years since the plates had been used the formulae for the inks used in printing – red, black, cyan (blue) and yellow – had changed subtly. The main change was to red; printing with 1962 blocks, using 1977 standard inks, would produce pictures that were not faithful to the original book plates. The difference was subtle, but would have been spotted by the specialists to whom the colours of the uniforms were specific and it was essential for them to be accurate. What had to be arranged was liaison with the ink manufacturer, and their laboratory technicians had to re-make inks especially for this printing job according to the original formulae.

After all of this, I am glad to say that that edition of the book was immensely successful, and one side benefit of it was that it brought me into contact with Bob Pigeon. Bob Pigeon was for a period publisher of the military publishing house Combined Publishing in the United States. However in 1978 he was in charge of production in New York at George Blagowidow's Hippocrene, who undertook the US co-publication of *The Anatomy of Glory*. It was from our getting to know each other at Hippocrene that our long relationship was established. Greenhill distributed Bob Pigeon's Combined books for a number of years, which continued until he sold the list to the Perseus Books Group and the name ceased to be used.

The Arms & Armour Press edition published in 1978 sold out, and a new printing of the book was undertaken in 1997, for which Colonel John Elting provided a new introduction. With technology moving on, the new edition was produced by offset lithography in South East Asia. For this edition the plates from the first edition from 1961 were compared to the reprint that was undertaken in 1962, and compared again to the 1978 edition, and then back to the original plates held in the Anne S. K. Brown Collection at Brown University. It was established that those from the second 1962 edition had been most faithful to the original items themselves, and it was these that were used for the Greenhill Books' reissue.

Yesteryear when working in type, problems occurred when authors needed to make changes, and this entailed bumping type through dozens of pages in order to find room for the new material. This was a deceptively costly process, but there was a certain logic to it. Nowadays it is very easy to change the content, but there are wholly different problems that can occur with computer programmes and typesetting.

22

SPECIAL PROJECTS

EVERY BOOK IS SPECIAL, with different and interesting aspects, but some books are more special than others.

One of the most thrilling projects in my publishing career was that of the publication of *Napoleon's Elite Cavalry.*

A letter came to us in May 1998 from a gentleman from whom we had not heard before, suggesting that we undertake a uniform project about the Napoleonic Wars in full colour. Publishers are always somewhat hesitant where full colour is concerned because of the considerable cost, but I arranged to meet him when, coincidentally, I was going to be in Washington DC just a few weeks later. The gentleman was Edward Ryan, and the wonderful colour artwork he was talking about was that by the master French military artist Lucien Rousselot. From what he showed me I was immediately interested, but extremely hesitant. I was immediately interested because there was a precedent for the successful publication of a book of Napoleonic uniforms in full colour. This was the two-volume *Napoleonic Uniforms*, which presented illustrations by Knötel, with descriptions by John Elting, which had been released by us in 1993 and was an outstanding success. I was frustrated and hesitant because of the cost implications.

Then things moved quickly.

The arrangements for my US tour included visiting the Anne S. K. Brown Military Collection in Providence, Rhode Island, just a couple of days after meeting with Edward Ryan. The Anne S. K. Brown Military Collection was the home of the Rousselot plates and their curator, Mr Peter Harrington, was able to show me the complete sequence. I was stunned. They were thrilling. They represented the finest work on a strong subject that was obviously very commercial. But how to undertake the project? We sat in their library and had a discussion, and the model I had in mind was the books by Guy Dempsey which had been published by Arms & Armour Press. I wasn't sure how well they had sold, and they were less than £20. Obviously the Rousselot plates could not be published at such a price. So although I immediately fell in love with the material, I was at that time – but only for a short while – still very hesitant. What changed the whole approach was that Peter Harrington's colleague, Bob Kenny, took away a selection of the plates to colour photocopy for me in order to enable me to take them away. He returned with the example plates each presented on large A3 paper, and it was as though there was a sudden and blinding flash of light. 'That's it!' I said. 'The way to do this project is as a large, special-format volume.'

That may have been the concept, but again, undertaking such a format, in full colour throughout, would have very significant cost implications.

I flew from Providence to New York, and met with some of the key people with whom we work. These meetings had of course all been set up in advance, and it was something of a coincidence that I was able to go from Washington to Providence and then to New York (the story might have been rather different, and certainly the time-scale would have been, if it had been the other way around). As I showed the colour photocopies to our key associates they met with universal acclaim. Nancy Whitin and Kathleen McDermott at the History Book Club immediately expressed very keen interest in taking a quantity for their members (and they had used a small quantity of *Napoleonic Uniforms*). So too did Michael Stephenson of Doubleday's Military Book Club. Greg Oviatt of the Barnes & Noble Catalog expressed enthusiasm. And so did Bill Corsa of Specialty Book Marketing. Bill Corsa, who, with Peter Sherred, I knew from Arco days, had been pivotal in the success of *Napoleonic Uniforms*, and saw the new project as being comparable.

With these five knowledgeable people offering support for the project (but not commitment), I returned to London to show my colleagues the material and undertake the costings. Which were difficult. But again we had in mind the success of *Napoleonic Uniforms*.

To go back to the beginning, in the early 1990s, Charlie Smith, the publisher of academic reference books at Macmillan, New York, told me that a collection of Knötel plates had been located, all original artwork. I expressed extreme caution. I had never heard of there being unpublished artwork by Knötel, who worked at the end of the nineteenth century, and early twentieth, and told him to take care and to check carefully just what he was being offered. The next time I was in New York he had a locked, steel, fireproof attaché case in his office, and opened it to show me a selection of the plates. They were thrilling, and I immediately offered encouragement and support for the project that became *Napoleonic Uniforms*. The 'Knötel' in this case was Richard,, the son of Herbert Knötel.

I offered encouragement and support, but not a commitment. The production of the book raised all sorts of problems for Macmillan, and they were not able to share material with us on a normal basis to facilitate co-edition publication. When the following year I was in New York, Charlie Smith showed me an advance set. I fell in love with it, but it was priced $250 and this raised a question as to which bookshops would dare stock it. I committed to 300 sets, nevertheless, and hand carried a set back to Britain with me. When I showed them to the then Greenhill Sales Manager, David Farnsworth, and said that we would have to sell them at £125, he thought I was totally out on a limb (if not my mind), and well past anything of which we, or in fact possibly the entire British book trade, had had experience. He could see how wonderful the work was physically, but quite rightly pointed out that no general bookshop would dream of subscribing and stocking two volumes priced £125. We proceeded with our announcements, by which time the price was £150 per set. The response was electrifying. The specialist booksellers, both in Britain and internationally, were extraordinarily enthused, and *Napoleonic Uniforms* sold extraordinarily well. In total Greenhill sold 1,100 sets, and could have sold more if the book had not sold out and been impractical to reprint.

Hence we had a precedent that there was a market for colour plates on the Napoleonic Wars, and also we had indications of enthusiasm from some key customers.

A special 282 x 222mm format (16 inches by 12 inches) for the proposed new book which was to become *Napoleon's Elite Cavalry* was created and discussed with the printers in South East Asia, a dummy was made and displayed at that year's Frankfurt Book Fair and, again, the response from the specialist customers was extremely enthusiastic, and we were able to commit to undertake the project.

Because we had managed to get the key players in the marketplace interested (and by that time James Opie of Britain's Military Book Club) we then had to proceed with real speed. Edward Ryan set to finishing his text, and from his point of view he had waited some while to be able to undertake this project and then had to do all the writing within a very short period. Printing was undertaken in South East Asia and the book was ready and released in September 1999. Its publication was greeted with acclaim.

Having established a methodology we followed it with: *Historic Sail*, which had plates by Joseph Wheatley, who sent them through the mail, entirely unsolicited, and text by Stephen Howarth; and *With Napoleon in Russia*, which was created from material in the Anne S. K. Brown Military Collection and for which the knowledgeable Greenhill editor Jonathan North translated Faber du Faur's original text and added an introductory essay. Next will be *Wellington's Army*, also based on the Anne S. K. Brown Military Collection and presenting in a large format the plates by the British military artist from the early nineteenth century, Charles Hamilton Smith, and to which the extremely knowledgeable military historian Philip Haythornthwaite has added text.

23

LITIGATION

ADVICE CONCERNING LITIGATION was once given by a barrister who said 'If a man threatens to steal your watch, punch him on the nose. If a man threatens to sue you for your watch, give it to him gladly and consider yourself out of the thing, and cheaply so.' Life isn't as simple as that, however.

Inevitably legal problems occur from time to time, sometimes of a commercial nature, and anyone involved in business may find these arise. One always has to be cognisant of the legal background of things when signing contracts with authors, or distributors, and to be sure to be clear in what is being said. For publishers legal problems on matters such as libel or copyright may also occur.

I am glad to say that I have had few enough contentious situations over the years, but when they do occur they can be extremely time-consuming and aggravating, and what may be regarded as justice to the layman is not necessarily justice in the eyes of the law.

In terms of legal matters pertaining to publishing the most immediate and obvious is copyright. We have always been very careful in researching the copyright situation when reprinting a long-out-of-print book, and locating the copyright holder. There have been three cases where we have located a copyright holder and prepared to publish a book, when out of the blue another and infringing edition has been announced, even appeared. These have been cases where the other publisher had not been able to locate the author's estate, and decided to take a risk. Unfortunately in one such case we had to have the publisher stash the whole edition of the book they had printed in their cellar, and they were permitted to hold it until we sold out of our edition and rights might have reverted. That occurred a decade or so ago, and unfortunately our edition has proved an extremely slow seller and that publisher still has the unsold books. In another case we took over the publisher's stock, fortunately for him at his cost price, and in the third were able to stop the publication of the infringing edition.

A dramatic situation occurred with 'parallel importing'. This is the very tricky situation where books are published in the United States and go on to the Continent of Europe, possibly through a wholesaler, and then come into Britain. This happens when sterling is highly valued against the dollar, because then American book prices seem (usually temporarily) low and people seek to take advantage of it. A situation arose when the dollar softened to an incredible \$2.50/£1, and the British book trade was in danger of having its exclusive copyright licences eroded by means of parallel importing. We had the licence on a range of books that we were distributing. The books originated in the United States, and at that time my Hampstead High Street offices had a very large remainder bookshop close by in which, suddenly, a pile of books for which we had an exclusive licence appeared. We had been in touch with the owner of the shop over some petty parallel importing, but now the heap of about thirty books caused us affront. We contacted the owner who laughingly said we should write to his solicitors, and obviously we were going to get a complete run-around. Hence we arranged a 'hit squad' and a small team of us went into the shop at a quiet time. I engaged the cashier in conversation, whilst a colleague or two went and picked up the stock of the book that was causing offence and marched out of the door with them. Whereupon I gave the cashier a receipt saying that they were being removed but held pending clearance of the copyright.

Nothing happened.

This fascinated me, and a month or two later at the Frankfurt Book Fair when the shop owner came by, he said, again laughingly, 'I knew that problem would sort itself out and we sold the books before you could do anything.' I gently queried the situation. I questioned why his cashier had not told him that we had removed the books, without paying. He was not happy. In fact he started jumping up and down a bit, frothing at the mouth.

We quickly received a letter from his solicitor, accusing us of theft. I advised that we were holding the books pending resolution of the copyright situation. I also advised the Publishers Association as to how we had endeavoured to sort out the matter, and they were astonished; nobody deals with a copyright situation like this, they exclaimed.

I offered to place the books in the hands of a third party, pending resolution, and was happy that the person who was now getting concerned in the matter, and who was now being caused aggravation, wasn't Arms & Armour Press as the shop owner had intended, but himself. After a couple of letters were exchanged, the whole matter was left and the books stayed in our storage until after the shop went out of business. The owner had caused so much aggravation with his parallel importing that publishers declined to offer him regular remainders that he would have been free to sell.

I have only had one case of libel arise, which was most fortunately headed off. After our publication of a reprint of the book *Storm From The Sea* by Peter Young we received a letter, in a crabbed handwriting, saying:

'I take grave exception to certain comments in your books ... referring to Chapter IV (Dieppe) there are a number of omissions and inaccuracies concerning my part in the attack on the German battery. These false and misleading paragraphs gravely impugn my military reputation and are defamatory.

Inter alia, but in particular I refer to [etc. etc.]

I categorically deny making any such suggestion. I am considering my position and any legal implications that might be involved.'

We phoned one of our friends at the Commando Association, and who had provided advice and help where the reprinting of this book was concerned. He was immediately sympathetic. He knew the person who was making the complaint, and said that there was indeed a possible bone of contention. The person making the complaint was however fairly old, not in good health and therefore often somewhat irascible. However we were advised that he was also a High Court judge, knew the law and would be able to take more action against us than we could afford, in terms of paying lawyers to handle the matter. Another aspect of the situation was that Peter Young had died, and therefore we could not review the matter with him, and so too shortly thereafter did Peter Young's wife.

We started a 'hearts and minds' campaign. We wrote with apologies, and asking for information so as to better understand the situation. A number of letters ensued, as we followed up what the complainant was writing about. We were also gently pointing out the problems of the delay in dealing with the situation, because he had not complained when the book was originally published some twenty years prior, but also fortunately our own edition was at that time on the point of selling out and there was no practical means to reach the copies in circulation. Eventually we established a certain rapport, and agreed that should we ever decide to reprint the book we would further review the situation with him, independently research the matter, and possibly adjust what was being said or provide a dissenting note by him, or additional evidence, in a new printing. When we recently came to make a decision about a reprint of the book we checked and discovered that indeed the complainant has now passed away, and without him we can't seek to investigate the situation that had made him so unhappy.

We have had two cases where we have gone to arbitration, one with an author who did not deliver acceptable material although he had received a large (too large) advance, and one against another publisher. With the author we felt aggrieved because of how he had tried to fob us off, and then in his evidence to the umpire he had libelled us. Although we won, we didn't receive any money, and bankrupted him. In the other case, the author of a book that we were licensing from another publisher to reprint also rewrote that book and had sold it to a publisher in Spain, apparently without anyone's knowledge. When we came to reissue the volume we found that we were in conflict in the marketplace with another version of the same book for the Spanish volume had separately been sold for translation into English. We objected to this, and went to arbitration, but we lost because it turned out, and without our knowledge, that the publisher who was sub-licensing to us did not have the usual exclusivity to rights to the author's material. We think that the decision against us was incorrect, but one cannot appeal an umpire's decision and at some stage one has to let go and move on.

24

THE BUSINESS OF
PUBLISHING

AT THE TIME THAT I SOLD ARMS & ARMOUR PRESS in October 1984 I was involved in three businesses: Arms & Armour Press, Ken Trotman and, together with my partner Clive Bingley, the London Book Fair. Clive and I first met in the early 1960s when I was with Herbert Jenkins. Jenkins handled the sale and distribution of the books being published by Kenneth Mason's eponymous imprint, and this led to my liaising with their manager, Clive Bingley. After Clive left Kenneth Mason to set up his own specialist, eponymous imprint, a very rare occurrence in those days, we remained in touch, and a few years later he undertook the invoicing and despatching of the first Arms & Armour Press books, taking over after our initial troubles with invoicing. This led to a continuing relationship, and partnership in a number of projects, over many years.

Following the sale of Arms & Armour Press to Link House Books, a few months later I sold the Ken Trotman business to Richard Brown, its knowledgeable Manager. Meanwhile Clive Bingley felt that it was time to sell the London Book Fair and we did so to Industrial & Trade Fairs shortly after the Fair held in March 1985. In commercial terms it was a slightly unusual transaction because there was no physical asset.

Clive suggested that we continue our long-standing association either by backing or buying other publishers. The first that we bought was Charles Griffin, a small STM ('scientific, technical and medical') publisher with eighteenth-century origins. We bought it from the seventh generation of the publishing family, but the list had long since fallen on hard times and was in a downward spiral. When I showed the catalogue to my brother Barry, one of Britain's top statisticians, whose degree at Cambridge was in computer science, he perused it and said that he expected to find Babbage's original book about the computer still listed as valid. We cut back and focused on Griffin's unique specialization in academic statistics. It soon however became apparent that to be viable as an STM publisher one had to publish at least 100 or so books a year, which called for more commitment than we had. Hence after an interesting eighteen months developing the list and its international distribution, we sold Griffin to Hodder Arnold.

Meanwhile in the Summer of 1985 I had a social lunch with John Taylor, whom I had known since we were both members of the Society of Young Publishers. He was Managing Director of Lund Humphries Publishers, and my Arms & Armour Press had done some work with him. Over lunch he advised that Lund Humphries was for sale. Clive and I stepped in and bought this well-known specialist art history publisher, which had been publishing since the 1940s, with John Taylor's essential continuing involvement which had begun in 1959. We greatly expanded the publishing list, which included a long-standing relationship with the Henry Moore Foundation. John Taylor, too, has had a long career in publishing, and is a gentleman of considerable practical knowledge, urbane and full of wisdom. Clive continued to be my partner until 1992, when he retired and sold his half to me. In 1999 I ensured the continuity of Lund Humphries Publishers by selling it to Ashgate.

For most of the transactions in which Clive Bingley was involved he favoured using the services of one of the large, City firms of solicitors. I much preferred, wherever possible and certainly where it was one of my own transactions, to use my long-standing solicitor Stephen Rayner, for personal service, professionalism and practicality.

All the transactions that I have been involved with have been cash-based. That simplifies things considerably. When I was in the process of selling Arms & Armour Press to Link House

Books, and at an advanced stage of the negotiation, they offered me shares at a special reduced rate. I demurred; I wasn't transferring an asset which I had spent years building up for somebody else's paper. About six weeks later, and of course they knew this when they were offering me their paper, Link House was itself bought, and the value of their shares multiplied significantly. I still thought however that I had made the right decision.

Being involved with the sale or purchase of a business is a fascinating process. It is usually conducted under great pressure, and the commercial and legal requirements are such that all sorts of information and documentation have to be produced, sometimes seemingly without reason but to support legal requirements of the facts of the situation. Mountains of paperwork can be built up.

Fortunately those transactions that I have been involved with have been agreed, and once a draft sale document has been produced I have always sought to short-circuit layers of query and debate between the sides by arranging for the principals from both sides to get together in a solicitor's conference room, together with their legal advisers and possibly also accountants, and spend however long is necessary to hammer out the clear meaning of everything and to formalise things. Such a meeting can last many hours, and if there is a dull time I look around the conference table at the two teams and try and add up the per hour rate of all the advisers. Such meetings are like an enormously expensive taxi meter, a gold plated meter with increments by the minute. But they get things done.

For one transaction the other side's solicitors fielded a litigation solicitor rather than a commercial lawyer. He was the legal equivalent of a pit bull terrier. Although it was an agreed transaction the litigation solicitor chose to test our lawyer aggressively on every point. Because it was an agreed transaction our legal advisers had sent over a good but young man, who stood his ground quietly whilst under increasing attack. The atmosphere became colder and colder. From time to time the senior partner of the other side popped into the room and finally I got up, took him to one side in the corridor, which certainly was not correct practice, to tell him that the approach his person was taking was such as to imperil the whole deal. There was another private chat, and the attitude changed after that, and it was downhill all the way.

Another transaction was being negotiated on an extremely hot day. However when the whole team, including the principals, is gathered together, people are not able to go out and get fresh air. One may leave the conference room for the calls of nature, but not otherwise. After a very long day, which had started at 7.30 am, at about 3.00 pm, the solicitors left the room to finalise the documentation. Family members on the other side then started bickering. Tempers started getting short, and a family member who had played no part in the business over the years due to his ill health and heart condition started to go red in the face and argue with his brother. We were all embarrassed but also concerned. What would happen if something happened to the red-faced family member, whose signature was necessary on the documentation? We did not know where to look, but fortunately solicitors returned to the office, conversation changed, and the documentation was signed.

The sale and acquisition of businesses is a fascinating, usually pressured process. I have been fortunate in having excellent professional advisers but there is no doubt that I much prefer the business of publishing itself.

IS THERE A MESSAGE?

MUCH THAT I HAVE WRITTEN ABOUT IN THESE PAGES is minutiae, some of it from a long time ago. I guess that with a personal interest in and sense of history, the history of my career thus far causes me to set down detail, often unique, about publishing that only I can recall, and possibly only of interest to me. However, setting down the journey of my career is a good way to look for a pattern (and some of the fun that one has had along the route), and to understand how one has arrived at the present.

In nearly fifty years of continual change it has been exciting to try and keep up with what surrounds sufficiently to stay in touch, to steer a central course, and not to go off on the many tangents, and illusory developments, that have been offered. My career has spanned from the printing of books by letterpress, little changed since Gutenberg, to computer technology; from books being a primary means of entertainment, and source of knowledge, to one of many; from publishing for sales in the geographically small area of Great Britain, to publishing for the world and English being the lingua franca.

I would venture to suggest that for the last half century of social, business and professional change one has needed a stable inner gyroscope, and personally I have always sought to do unto others as I would wish them to do unto me.

A new and exciting era is dawning, especially as the many ways to use computers evolve, but publishers will still have a key role to play, human nature has not changed, and what is past is prologue.

Part Two of *On Publishing* will continue with the story of Greenhill Books in the 1990s, and the next two decades.

INDEX

ABA (BEA) 80, 102-3, 129-32, 135-9
Adams & Dart 118
Allan, Hugh 104
American Booksellers Assocation Convention, *see* ABA
Anatomy of Glory, The 84, 184-6
Ancient Scottish Weapons 113
Anderson, John 75
Annals of Hampstead, The 47
Anne S. K. Brown Military Collection 176, 186, 187, 190-1
Annis, P. G. W. 75
Antique European & American Firearms in the Hermitage Museum 62
Arab-Israeli Wars, The 85, 161, 162
Architectural Press, The 118
Arco, New York 26, 35, 38, 71-2, 130, 189
Armour of Imperial Rome, The 82
Armoury of Windsor Castle, The 113
Armoury of the Castle of Churburg, The 113
Arms & Armour Press 8, 28, 35-46, 51, 54, 56, 72, 75-80, 81, 89, 91, 92, 94, 96, 97 98-9, 113, 114, 117, 118, 121, 133, 140, 145, 146, 148, 149, 150, 151, 164, 185, 186, 188, 195, 199, 200
Arms and Armour Press Illustrated Monographs 38
Ashgate Publishing Ltd 200
Atkinson, Rosemary 22, 97
Atlas of Military Strategy 82

Austin, Paul Britten 159
Australian Bookseller and Publisher 125
Autopress Ltd 118

Bader, Douglas 84
Badges of the British Army 41-42
Baier, Marianne 79
Barbican, London 124, 125, 126-7
Barnes and Noble, NY 188
Barrie and Jenkins 23
Barrie and Rockcliffe 22, 23
Battles of the Bible 163, 164
Bayonets 39
BEA, see ABA
Beckwith, Charles A., Colonel 85, 143
Bennett, Don 84
Bernard & Graefe, Germany 49
Berry, Leigh Ann 80, 102
Bertelsmann 23
Bewick, Thomas 150
Bibliography and Readers' Guide to the First Editions of P. G. Wodehouse, A 18
Bingley, Clive 40, 54, 118, 119, 120, 121, 125, 126, 127, 181, 199, 200
Bison Books 56
Blackmore, Howard L. 26, 181
Blagowidow, George, 186
Blair, Claude 26, 114
Blandford Press Ltd 54, 78, 88, 118, 127, 199, 200
Bomber Harris: His Life and Times 84
Bomber Offensive 84, 154
BookExpo America, *see* ABA
Bookseller, The 19, 54, 55, 120, 125, 129, 130-1, 143
Brave Men's Blood: The

Epic of the Zulu War, 1879 155
Brewer, Vicki 80
British and American Tanks of World War II 38, 41
British Battleships of the Second World War 82, 145, 147
British Cruisers of the Second World War 82, 145
British Medical Association 133
British Military Firearms 26, 28
British Military Uniforms 82
British Pistols and Guns 37
British Smooth-Bore Artillery 41
British Tank Markings and Names 74
Brown, Anne S. K., *see* Anne S. K. Brown
Brown, David 154, 181
Brown, Richard and Roz 91, 94, 96, 99, 114-5, 199
Brown University Press, USA 184
Butterflies of the World 56, 86, 184

Caesar's Palace, Las Vegas 138
Cairncross, Sue 105
Callas, Maria 22
Campaign of Waterloo, The 153, 166
Carew, Tim 166-8
Carman, W. Y. 27
Cass, Frank, & Co. Ltd 118
Cassell & Co. Ltd 150
Catalogue of European Court Swords 113
Catalogue of European Daggers 113
Catch-22 38

Index

Century Publishing Co. Ltd 23
Chamberlain, Peter 38, 41, 76, 82
Champagne From My Slipper 21
Chandler, David G. 82, 83-4, 108, 136, 153, 159
Channel Press, NY 70
Childs Hill, London 35, 41, 46
Chilton, Charles 12
CIA 156
Clancy, Tom 132, 145-148
Clematis Press Ltd 118
Coffey, Edward 57, 101
Colledge, J. J. 153
Collins, William, Sons and Co. Ltd 126, 146, 148,
Colt, Harris 180
Combat Aircraft of World War II 82
Combined Publishing, USA 186
Commando Men 153
Cooper, Leo, Ltd 118, 172
Corsa, Bill 101, 188
Covent Garden 9, 30
Crosby Lockwood and Son Ltd 118
Crown, New York 35, 38

Daily Mail, London 141
Daily Mirror, London 29, 33
Darth Vader 129, 131
Davis, Brian L. 42, 82
Dawsons of Pall Mall 118
DBI Books 25, 72, 75, 92
Dean, Bashford 113
Delta Force 85, 143
Dempsey, Guy 188
Desert Storm 157
Detweiler, David 79, 80
Devin-Adair, NY 70
Dickens, Peter 143, 181
Dickenson, Mike 27
Dictionary of Military Terms 153
Doenitz: Memoirs - Ten Years and Twenty Days 154
Dorling Kindesley Ltd 53
Doyle, Arthur Conan 152
Doyle, Hilary L. 82
Drexler, Susan 80
Drownproofing 21

Drummond, James 113
Duke of York Street, London 15, 16, 18
Duell, Sloan & Pearce, NY 70
Duffy, Christopher 159
Dunn & Bradstreet 72
Dupuy, Trevor N. 157

Eagle, T. W. 15, 23, 70, 72, 97
Early Breech-Loaders 36
Early Percussion Firearms 26, 28
Eccles, Lord David 119
Edgware, Middlesex 8, 12, 36
Ellis, Chris 38, 41, 76, 82
Elstree and Borehamwood Through Two Thousand Years 47
Elting, John, Colonel 110, 159, 174-8, 181, 186, 187
Emery Medical Center, Atlanta 132-133
EMI 30
Emperor's Press, Chicago 175
Encyclopedia of German Tanks of World War Two, The 82
Encyclopedia of Infantry Weapons of World War II, The 56
Encyclopedia of World Stamps 86
English, Irish and Scottish Firearms Makers 37
Epley, Kevin 146
Epley, Thomas 77, 146
Erickson, John, 181
Essenwein, A. 113
Ethell, Jeffrey L. 110, 159, 178-180, 181
Etterlin, von Senger und 38, 41, 75
Evans, Anthony Arthur 41, 99, 151
Evans, Jean-Marc 105
Evelyn, Hugh 118
Exercise of Armes, The 153
Export Credit Guarantee Dept 36
Ezell, Edward C. 181

Faber and Faber, Ltd 50
Farnsworth, David 189
Farren, Irving 97

Fawcett, NY 70
Fell, Frederick, NY 70
Few Quick Ones, A 18
ffoulkes, Charles 37
Finchley Road, North West London 8, 41, 44, 45
Firearms Investigation, Identification and Evidence 75
Firepower 42
Fleet Publishing, NY 70
Fleming, Adrian 80
Flintlock Pistols 75
Folio Society, The 119
Follett, USA 72
Fontana 141
Fopp, Dr. Michael 107
Forsyth, Frederick 172
Fortescue, John, Sir 153, 166
Fortnum & Mason 20
Frankfurt Book Fair 21, 27, 49-51, 53-9, 78, 79, 88, 101, 120, 123, 124, 128, 155, 156, 190, 194
Frewin, Anthony 47
Frost, David 73
Fuehrer Conferences on Naval Affairs 154

Gas, Air and Spring Guns of the World 75, 77
Geis, Bernard, NY 70
Gendarme, Judic 105
Geraghty, Tony 81, 139-143
German Army Uniforms & Insignia 42, 82
German Navy in World War II, The 145
German Pistols and Revolvers 75
German Tanks of World War II 38, 41, 42, 75
Gibbons, David 41, 99, 151
Gichon, Mordechai 159, 163
Gill, John H., Colonel 111, 159
G.I. Victory 180
Gladstone, Milton 35, 37, 71-72, 130
Globus, Rudo, NY 70
Godden, Geoffrey 23
Great Frankfurt Campaigns 58
Great Patriotic War, The 65

Greener, W. W. 37
Greenhill Books 8, 20, 26, 41, 78, 79, 101, 118, 135, 143, 149, 150-9, 164, 186, 189
Greenhill Napoleonic Wars Data Book, The 174
Gregg International Publishers Ltd 119
Greiffenagen, Maurice 20
Griffin, Charles 199-200
Griffith, Paddy 111, 159
Grimsdick, J. Derek 15, 22, 23, 69, 70, 72, 97
Grosset and Dunlap, NY 70
Grosvenor, Deborah 147
Grosvenor Hotel, London 121, 123, 125
Guinness Book of Records 14
Gun and its Development, The 37
Gun Digest 72, 75

Hamilton Smith, Charles 191
Hamlyn, Paul 23, 29-34, 35, 38, 92
Hampstead High Street, London 35, 46, 63, 81, 96, 99, 149, 194
Handel Smithy Bookshop, Edgware 8, 11-14
Hanna, Bill 57, 138
Harrington, Peter 187
Harris, Sir Arthur 84, 154
Hartigan, Charles T. 72
Hastings House, NY 70
Hatchards, London 15, 21
Hatcher, Julian S., General 75
Hatcher's Notebook 75
Haythornthwaite, Philip 191
Hearthside Press, NY 70, 71
Herbert Jenkins Ltd 9, 12, 14, 15, 16, 18, 20, 22, 23, 25, 26, 27, 28, 30, 35, 37, 49, 61, 69, 71-2, 75, 91, 92, 97, 181, 199
Hermitage, Leningrad 62, 68
Herzog, Chaim 85, 109, 159, 161-4, 181
High Flyers 172
High Hill Bookshop, Hampstead 81, 94

Hill and Wang, NY 70
Hippocrene Books, NY 186
Historic Sail 190
History Book Club, USA 188
History of the Art of War, A 153
History of the British Army, A 166
History of Spanish Firearms, A 26, 28
Hofschröer, Peter 159
Hogg, Ian V. 44-45, 56, 75, 77, 82, 109, 159
Holt, Henry, NY 136
Horward, Donald D. 153
Howarth, Stephen 190
Hughes, B. P. 'Bil', Major General 41, 42, 181
Hunt, Ralph Vernon 29
Hunt for Red October, The 145-148
Hurlbutt, William 177
Hutchinson Publishing Group Ltd 23

If War Comes 157
Illustrated Encyclopedia of Handguns, The 66
Illustrated Napoleon, The 136
Immelmann: The Eagle of Lille 151
Imperial War Museum 42
Industrial & Trade Fairs 127, 199
Infantry Attacks 74
Inside the SAS 143
Intercontinental Hotel, London 120, 123
Intrepid, NY 134, 135
Invasion: The German Invasion of England, July 1940 85
In Zululand 153
IPC 29, 31
Isby, David C. 159, 180

Japanese Armour 75
Japanese Arms and Armour 42
Jarvis, Philip 29, 30, 32
Jasen, David A. 18, 23
Jeeves in the Offing 18
Jenkins, Herbert, see Herbert Jenkins Ltd
Jentz, Thomas 82
Jermyn Street, London 15, 16

Johns, Glenn 79
Johnson, Johnnie (Group Captain J. E.) 84
Jones, Lynda 99, 105, 151
Journal of a Regimental Officer 114
Journal of the Waterloo Campaign, The 152
Journey into Space 12, 14
Julian Press, NY 70

Kane, Richard 134
Kane, Robert V., Colonel 106, 132
Kennedy Shaw, W. B. 154
Kenny, Robert W., Jr. 188
Kindersley, Peter 53
Kissinger, Henry 63
Konyn, Gerald 11, 13, 14
Knight, Ian 108, 155, 159
Knotel, Herbert 175, 187, 189
Krause, Iola 72, 77
Kronberg, Germany 52, 55, 58, 78, 100, 146
Kruger, Helen and Peter 61

Lachouque, Henri 83
Ladd, James 143
Laking, Guy Francis 113, 114
Langellier, John 159
Latham, John 36
Lavin, James 26
Law, D. G. 154
Lee-Enfield Rifle, The 25, 26, 27, 28
Leningrad 62, 63, 68
Letts, Charles, Ltd 35
Leventhal, Barry 199
Leventhal, Elizabeth 46, 67-8, 76-7, 99, 104-5
Leventhal, Louise 163
Leventhal Medical Video 133
Lewis, Cecil 107, 159, 171-4, 181
Library Association, The 117, 119
Link House Books Ltd 54, 78, 88, 149, 150, 199, 200-1
London Arms Fair 39, 100
London Book Fair 54, 58, 80, 117-128, 131, 199
London Library 20
Longman Group Ltd 126

Index

Long Range Desert Group 154
Lord of the Rings, The 12
Lost Victories 153
Lovat Scouts 169
Lucas, James 42, 112, 159
Luger 82
Lund Humphries
 Publishers Ltd 20, 54,
 119, 184, 200

Macksey, Kenneth 74, 85,
 111, 159
McDermott, Kathleen 188
Macmillan, NY 175, 189
Majendie, V. D. 36
Manstein, Erich von, Field
 Marshal 153
Mann, J. G. 113
*Manual for Air Raid
 Warden Instruction* 113
Marine Life 86
Martin, Paul 26
Marx Brothers 152
Maxwell, Robert 12
Mayer, Sidney 56
McCormack, Sue 104-5
*Memoirs of Field-Marshal
 Kesselring, The* 153
Mercer, General Cavalié
 152
Messner, Julian, NY 70
*MHQ: The Quarterly
 Journal of Military
 History* 135
Military Book Club 83,
 188, 190
Military Book Show
 133-135
*Military Breech-Loading
 Small Arms* 36
Military Costume 26, 28
Military History (USA) 135
*Military History and Atlas
 of the Napoleonic Wars*
 176
*Military Lessons of the
 Gulf War* 157
*Military Maxims of
 Napoleon, The* 153
*Military Pistols and
 Revolvers* 45
*Military Small Arms of the
 20th Century* 77, 82
Milsom, John 38, 42, 65
Modern Soviet Armour 82
Moorcock, Michael 17
Moran, Pat 80, 103
Motorbuch Verlag,

Germany 49
Museum of American Art,
 DC 137-8
Music for Pleasure 30

Napoleonic Fair,
 International 83, 176,
 177
Napoleonic Library 152,
 166
*Napoleonic Military
 History: A Bibliography*
 153
Napoleonic Uniforms 175,
 187, 189-190
Napoleon's Elite Cavalry
 187-190
Naval Institute Press 77,
 134, 145
Naval Swords 75
Newnes 29
New York 35, 69, 73, 129,
 132
Norman, A. V. B. 27, 39,
 82, 181
Norrie, Ian 81, 94, 96
North, Jonathan 105, 191

Obolensky, Ivan, NY 70
Octopus Publishing Group
 Ltd., The 126
Odhams Books 29
Oman, Sir Charles 153
Opie, James 103, 190
Orbach & Chambers 119
Orion Press, NY 70
Orion Publishing Group
 Ltd, UK 150
Osprey 78, 135
Outlet, NY 120
Oviatt, K. Gregory 102,
 188

Palmer, David 105
Penguin Books Ltd 17,
 126
*Perfection of Military
 Discipline, The* 113
Performing Flea 17
Philosophical Library, NY
 70
Pigeon, Robert L. 106,
 186
Plancey, Rabbi Alan 180
Planeta, Moscow 55
*Police Tactics in Armed
 Situations* 140
Polmar, Norman 134
Pope, Donna 79, 80, 103

Presidio Press, USA 79,
 134, 158
Price, Alfred, Dr 159
Primedia Enthusiast
 Publications 135
Probert, Henry 84
Publishing News 27
Publishers' Association
 121, 131, 195
Publishers Weekly 125

Queen, Ellery 152
*Quellen zur Geschichte fur
 Feuerwaffen* 113
Quill and Quire 125

Royal Air Force Museum
 84, 107, 169, 172
Random House, NY 151-2
Random House, UK 23
Rapiers 39, 75
*Rapier and Small Sword,
 The* 82
Raven, Alan 82, 145
Rayner, Stephen 200
*Record of European Arms
 and Armour* 113, 114
Red Air Fighter, The 151
Red Army Uniforms, 1944
 43
Rees, Gerry 15
Reiner, Joe 120
Reitmulder, Jim 79
Reynolds, E. G. B. 25
Ritter, David 80, 102
Roberts, John 82, 145
Robinson, H. Russell 27,
 42, 82
Rohwer, Jurgen 154,
 159
Rommel, Erwin, Field
 Marshal 74
Ronald Press, NY 70
Rossi, Peter 80, 103
Rovers of the Night Sky
 151
Rowe, Anthony 149
Royal Armouries 27, 42
Royal Artillery 44
Royal Artillery Institution
 42
*Royal Navy in World War
 II* 154
Royal United Services
 Institute 85, 92
*Russian Infantry Weapons
 of World War II* 61
Russian Tanks, 1900-1970
 38, 42, 65

On Publishing

Ryan, Edward 110, 187, 190
Ryle, Kate 105

Sagittarius Rising 107, 171, 172, 174
St. James's, London 9, 15, 16, 20
St. Petersburg 68
Samain, Bryan 153
SAS, *see* Special Air Service
SAS: The Jungle Frontier 143
SBS: The Invisible Raiders 143
Schnell, Judith 78-9, 80, 103
Scottish Swords and Dirks 75
Seaby, B. A., Ltd 119
Seafire: The Spitfire that Went to Sea, The 154
Secretaries of the Navy 147
Seeley, Service & Co. Ltd 119
Sherman, The 38
Sherred, Peter, 188
Ships of the Royal Navy 153
Shooting Times 25, 92
Shore, Clifford, Captain 168-170
Shotgun Marksmanship 25
Showell, Jak Mallman 145, 154
Silvester, Victor 17
Simkin Marshall Ltd 12
Simmons, Anthony J. 41
Simon, Andre L. 17
Skender, Edward, Colonel 80
Small Arms of the World 77
Small and Specialist Publishers' Exhibition, *see* SPEX
Smith, Charles Hamilton, 191
Smith, Charlie 189
Smith, Cordwainer 17
Smith, Digby 159, 174
Smith, W. H. B. 75
Society of Young Publishers, The 69, 200
Soviet Casualties and Combat Losses 61, 67
Soviet Trade Delegation 63-5

Soviet Wings 55, 66, 155-7
Special Forces Club 143
Specialty Book Marketing, NY 188
Specialist Publishers' Exhibition for Librarians 118
SPEX 119, 120
Spick, Mike 159
Stableford, Brian 150
Stackpole Books 25, 38, 72-3, 75-80, 92, 102-3, 135, 158
Stephens, Frederick J. 39
Stephenson, Michael 188
Sterling Books, NY 78
Stormbringer 17
Storm from the Sea 154, 195
Strachan, Hew 82
Strauss, John 72
Stuart, Cath 104
Summers, Montague 18
Sutton, Jim 134, 135, 146
Sword, Lance and Bayonet 37

Tanks of the World 76, 82
Tarassuk, Dr Leonid 62-65, 67, 68
Tarring, Andrew 104
Taylor, John A. 58, 102, 200
Things to do in the Woods with Brownies 17
Thorburn, W. A. 181
Thorsons Publishers Ltd 119
Tolkien, J. R. R. 12
Tower of London, HM 27, 42
Trapp, Oswald 113
Trotman, Ken 25, 35, 36, 37, 87, 91-95, 99, 113-5, 199
Trotman, Marie 91-2, 93
Tsouras, Peter G. 65, 111, 159
Tubb, E C 17
Tuck, Stanford 84
Tudor, NY 70

Uffindell, Andrew 159
United Nations 69, 161-2
United Newspapers 88
University Press, NY 70

Valentine, Eric 39, 40, 75
Valentine, Mitchell 119

Victoria & Albert Museum 26
Victorian Collector Series 17, 26
Vintage Crime Classics 150, 151
Vintage Science Fiction and Fantasy 150, 151

Wallace Collection 27, 39
Wallace, Edgar 150
Walter, John 41, 82, 108, 153
War of Atonement, The 164
Warbirds Illustrated 78
Warships of the Imperial Japanese Fleet, The 145
Wartels, Nat 35, 37, 38
Waterloo 83
Waterloo Day 83
Waterloo Roll Call 46
Watson, Bruce 157, 159, 181
Weal, Elke C. 82
Weal, John A. 82
Weeks, John 77
Weidenfeld & Nicolson Ltd 163
Weller, Jac 181
Wellington's Army 153
Wheatley, Joseph 190
Whitin, Nancy 188
Who Dares Wins 81, 87, 113, 140-143, 146
Wilkinson, Frederick J. 27, 42, 75
Wilson, Larry 62, 63, 85-6
Witherby, H. F. & G. 119
With Napoleon in Russia 190
Wodehouse, P. G. ('Plum') 17-18, 23
P.G. Wodehouse: The Portrait of a Master 18
Woolf, Jack 20
World Trade Center 74, 78
Wray, Mark 101, 104-5
Wyatt, R. J., Lieutenant Colonel 168

Yoseloff, Thomas, NY 70
Young, Peter, Colonel 154, 195-6

Zaloga, Steven 82
Zangwill, Israel 152
Zhuk, A. B. 66